T0316545

Cambridge Elements

Elements in Development Economics
Series Editor-in-Chief
Kunal Sen
UNU-WIDER and University of Manchester

ECONOMIC TRANSFORMATION AND INCOME DISTRIBUTION IN CHINA OVER THREE DECADES

Cai Meng
Minzu University of China

Bjorn Gustafsson
University of Gothenburg and IZA – Institute of Labor Economics

John Knight
University of Oxford and the Oxford Chinese Economy Programme (OXCEP)

Shaftesbury Road, Cambridge CB2 8EA, United Kingdom

One Liberty Plaza, 20th Floor, New York, NY 10006, USA

477 Williamstown Road, Port Melbourne, VIC 3207, Australia

314–321, 3rd Floor, Plot 3, Splendor Forum, Jasola District Centre, New Delhi – 110025, India

103 Penang Road, #05–06/07, Visioncrest Commercial, Singapore 238467

Cambridge University Press is part of Cambridge University Press & Assessment, a department of the University of Cambridge.

We share the University's mission to contribute to society through the pursuit of education, learning and research at the highest international levels of excellence.

www.cambridge.org
Information on this title: www.cambridge.org/9781009467933

DOI: 10.1017/9781009357616

First published 2023

A catalogue record for this publication is available from the British Library

ISBN 978-1-009-46793-3 Hardback
ISBN 978-1-009-35763-0 Paperback
ISSN 2755-1601 (online)
ISSN 2755-1598 (print)

Economic Transformation and Income Distribution in China over Three Decades

Elements in Development Economics

DOI: 10.1017/9781009357616
First published online: November 2023

Cai Meng
Minzu University of China

Bjorn Gustafsson
University of Gothenburg and IZA – Institute of Labor Economics

John Knight
University of Oxford and the Oxford Chinese Economy Programme (OXCEP)

Author for correspondence: Bjorn Gustafsson, bjorn.gustafsson@socwork.gu.se

Abstract: It is arguable that the most important event in the world economy in recent decades has been the rise of China, from being on a par with sub-Sahara Africa at the start of economic reform to being an economic superpower today. That rise remains under-researched. Moreover, the great structural changes which accompanied economic growth require examination. The nationally representative China Household Income Project (CHIP) surveys, conducted for the years 1988, 1995, 2002, 2007, 2013, and 2018, permit a detailed examination of many important aspects of a country's economic development. Much of the analysis of this Element is closely related to, and largely caused by, China's remarkable economic growth and income distribution over the thirty years. This title is also available as Open Access on Cambridge Core.

Keywords: economic transformation, income distribution, economic growth, labour market, China

ISBNs: 9781009467933 (HB), 9781009357630 (PB), 9781009357616 (OC)
ISSNs: 2755-1601 (online), 2755-1598 (print)

Contents

1 Introduction

It is arguable that the most important event in the world economy in recent decades has been the rise of China, from being poorer than sub-Saharan Africa at the start of economic reform to being an economic superpower today. That rise remains under-researched. Moreover, the great structural changes which accompanied economic growth require examination. In this case, the five published edited volumes that have resulted from the nationally representative China Household Income Project (CHIP[1]) surveys have been a major source for understanding the effects of economic growth on such issues as the labour market, poverty, and inequality (Griffin and Zhao, 1993; Riskin et al., 2001; Gustafsson et al., 2008; Li et al., 2013; Sicular et al., 2020, and issue 1 of the journal *China & World Economy*, 2022). The research based on CHIP has reached not only those who read texts in English but also Chinese language readers. Regarding the latter, papers have been collected in no less than twelve volumes (Li and Zhao, 2020).

These periodic surveys, conducted for the years 1988, 1995, 2002, 2007, 2013, and 2018, provide a great opportunity to trace this remarkable transformation. Not only did they have much design and information in common but also the surveyors adapted their questionnaires as the economy and therefore research questions evolved. This series of research-motivated surveys over a period of thirty years is unique for China and probably for the developing world.

1.1 CHIP by CHIP

The six CHIP surveys, spanning thirty years of headlong growth and transformation, permit a detailed examination of many important aspects of a country's economic development. The CHIP surveys each contains much common information about China's households and their income over time, but also on China's economic and social transformation. The combination of rapid economic growth and movement from a centrally planned to a market economy makes China the most interesting economy in the world. The connected but developing series of CHIP nationally representative surveys makes its evidence an ideal vehicle for understanding the evolving economy and society. The CHIP also provided inspiration for other efforts to collect economic information from households in China and thereby research based on it. Two close followers are the volumes edited by Li and Sato (2006), which focused on urban China, and by Gustafsson, Hasmath, and Ding (2021), which analysed ethnic disparities.

---

[1] Further information on CHIP can be found in the Appendix of this book.

The remaining paragraphs of this section explain how CHIP began, and what the first survey attempted to achieve, and how the questionnaires changed as the economy and society developed.

In 1988, microeconomic information on Chinese households was sadly lacking. The Institute of Economics of the Chinese Academy of Social Sciences initiated a new national survey, funded from local and foreign sources, to be designed and analysed by Chinese and foreign scholars. Being a sub-sample of the national survey of the National Bureau of Statistics (as it is now named), it drew on the NBS data but added many new questions with research hypotheses in mind. The main objective of the first survey was to obtain an accurate picture of household incomes in this still partly planned but marketising economy.

Subsequent surveys differed in objectives and in information. It was important to examine changes over time, so required the same set of questions in each survey. However, the emergence of new issues required new questions and new hypotheses. For instance, privatisation, urbanisation, rural–urban migration, diminishing poverty, increasing inequality, accumulating wealth, and new policy interventions, each needed attention. Beyond the core questions, the CHIP surveys evolved to answer the new questions.

1.2 Issues and Questions

Much of the analysis of this Element is closely related to, and largely caused by, China's remarkable economic growth over the thirty years. Without such rapid growth, our story would be very different. It is therefore important to understand from the outset how and why the economy has grown so rapidly. That is our first objective.

To what extent can the growth rate be explained by the sort of econometric analysis that economists conventionally use? What role does China's particular political economy play? How have incentives been harnessed in the pursuit of economic growth? What role did the great structural changes – including privatisation, trade, and industrialisation – play in both contributing to and resulting from economic growth? These are the questions which we attempt briefly to answer in Section 2. This section differs from the others in that it necessarily relies on macroeconomic and other evidence rather than the microeconomic household-based evidence provided by the CHIP surveys.

In 1988, workers in rural China were mainly self-employed farm workers, restricted in their mobility from the village. In Section 3, we take a close look at the development of employment in rural China from 1988 to 2018. We ask: why, when, and how rapidly did the flight from agriculture into wage employment and self-employment occur? What characterises those who are wage earners or self-employed and not farmers? Did the move increase income? Have the income consequences changed as more and more people moved out of farming?

In 1988, workers in urban China were employed in an administered labour system, with barely any scope for market forces to operate. By 2018, a great many rural *hukou* holders were wage-employed as migrant workers, involving 'the greatest migration in human history'. Most urban workers were now employed in competitive labour markets, although marketisation was by no means complete. There had been a vast change in the allocation, use, and remuneration of labour. How did this transformation come about?

How could labour market reform be achieved in the face of vested interests and the need for coordinating various interacting reforms, such as financial, enterprise, and housing reform? To what extent did the wage structure reflect the productivity of workers? Did the emergent labour market nevertheless remain segmented in various policy-related ways? These questions are the subject of Section 4.

Throughout the twentieth century, China was a labour surplus economy *par excellence.* The remarkable growth of the economy, and in particular the urban economy, required a great influx of labour into the cities and towns. The influx was accentuated by the slow growth of the urban-born labour force. There are now a very large number of rural persons working in urban locations.[2]

China's progress can be gauged against the famous Lewis model of a dual economy, in which economic growth occurs through the transfer of labour from the low-productivity rural (traditional) sector to the high-productivity urban (modern) sector at a market wage held down by surplus labour. Eventually, rural-born labour becomes scarce, migrant wages and rural incomes rise, and the economy moves from the classical to the neoclassical stage, in which the fruits of economic development become more widely spread. Between the two stages is a turning point.

The Lewis model has huge implications for the alleviation of poverty and the reduction of inequality. It is an important question: has China passed the turning point? Is the transfer of labour from rural to urban China and the ensuing tightening of the labour market the reason why the Gini coefficient of household income per capita rose throughout our period until about 2010, since when it has remained fairly stable? These are the key questions posed in Section 5.

During the planning epoque state-owned enterprises provided income support and heavily subsidised housing for urban workers and their household members. Urban households typically did not pay any income taxes. In contrast, members of the rural households, at that time predominantly farmers, had no access to social security benefits but had to pay taxes. Those situations have changed as China has taken steps towards a market economy. For example, the government has come to

---

[2] For issues on measuring the number of rural to urban migrants, see Section 5.2.

take a much more active role in regulating and providing pensions and, more recently, has done this also for rural households. In Section 6, we take a fresh look at how the redistributive effect of public expenditures and revenues in China changed from 1988 to 2018. This we do for China as a whole and also separately for households living in rural and urban areas.

In Section 7, we turn our interest to income inequality and wealth inequality during the period from 1988 to 2018. We ask: how have these inequalities changed over the three decades of institutional change and rapid economic growth? We are interested in changes in the inequality of the two distributions, and particularly in how the urban to rural income and wealth ratios have contributed to income inequality and wealth inequality. As a guide to understanding, we also ask whether changes have differed during various sub-periods.

We continue to look at how income is distributed across households in Section 8, but from two other angles. One is from the perspective of inequality of opportunities (IOp). This approach requires that measures of income inequality be separated into two parts: one that reflects inequality for which the individual should be held responsible and another due to factors beyond the individual's control. We report one attempt to quantify the two parts and this for the period 2002–18. Section 8 also focuses on people with lesser means: China's income-poor. We use official criteria to assess how the rural poverty rate changed from 2002 to 2018. However, when many households in urban China are approaching a standard of living prevailing in high-income countries, criteria for defining poverty similar to those used in such countries will become relevant. What consequences will this have for mapping the extent and profile of relative poverty among urban people?

When the Chinese Communist Party (CCP) came to power at the end of the 1940s, the new government brought ambitious ideas influencing policies regarding social rights for women, particularly those living in urban areas. The new government also had higher ambitions than the previous one regarding the situation of ethnic minorities. In Section 9, we look closely at how inequality along those two dimensions of the population has developed since the end of the 1980s. We ask: has the gender wage gap in urban China increased since the introduction of economic reform in the 1990s? If so, how can this increase be understood? On average do members of particular ethnic minorities have a less favourable economic outcome than do members of the Han majority?

As the Chinese economy has grown so rapidly, one can expect that an increased number of people now live lives similar to those in high-income countries. In Section 10, we examine the number and proportion of people who live in households, that, if they lived in EU countries, would be considered neither poor nor very well off? Where do those members of the middle class live and to what extent are they wage earners? Are people who grew up in urban

China more likely to be middle class than those who were rural-born, particularly those who have not migrated to an urban area? This new phenomenon has implications for market size and structure, but also sociopolitical implications. Finally, the contents of the various sections are summarised in Section 11.

1.3 Objectives and Methods

Our objective in this small volume is to provide a readable account of the remarkable effects of economic growth and transformation on China's households, drawing in particular on the evidence to be derived from the six CHIP national household surveys. The emphasis is on interest and understanding. The Element draws on the results of many technical or rigorous sections in the CHIP volumes or journal articles based on CHIP, several written by us. We assume that our readers are more interested in the main results rather than the methods by which they were obtained.

In addition to answering the many specific questions listed in Section 2, we shall – if and where appropriate – consider three general questions. First, why did China's progress on these issues differ from that of other comparable countries? Second, how do we contribute to the literature on China's progress? Third, how do we engage with controversies, for instance arising from different data sources?

We three authors are jointly responsible for this Element as a whole. Nevertheless, there has been some division of labour, corresponding to each's research interests and research publications. Thus, John Knight has taken the lead with Sections 2, 4, and 5. Bjorn Gustafsson has done so with Sections 3, 9, and 10. He and Meng Cai have jointly written Sections 6 and 7, and Meng Cai has taken primary responsibility for Section 8. All three of us have equally contributed to the Introduction (Section 1) and the Conclusion (Section 11).

2 Why Has China Grown So Fast?

2.1 Introduction

The transformation of China's economy and society over the economic reform period is primarily due to its rapid rate of economic growth, and to the various factors that made it possible. We draw on the book *China's Remarkable Economic Growth*, which attempted to explain why China had grown so fast (Knight and Ding, 2012). The annual growth rate of real gross domestic product (GDP) in China averaged 10.2 per cent in the decade 1980–90, 10.6 per cent in 1990–2000, and 10.3 per cent in 2000–7. Even after the global financial crash, China's growth rate was relatively unaffected, averaging 8.9 per cent per annum over the decade 2007–17. China is unique among large economies in maintaining very rapid growth for forty years.

The dramatic rise of China over such a short period of time is arguably the most important recent economic event in the world economy. It poses questions that deserve to be answered. Why did it happen? How did it happen? Can it continue? Does its experience carry lessons for other countries? Can the conventional empirical approach of economists to economic growth provide satisfactory answers? Are the underlying causes of growth, which in turn explain the variables that economists can measure, no less important? These questions are the subject of this section. They set the stage for our analyses of economic growth's socio-economic consequences to come in later sections.

2.2 Econometric Approaches

The approach to economic growth that economists conventionally adopt is by means of growth models and growth empirics. It was possible to analyse China's economic growth by means of a cross-country panel data set.[3] The actual annual average growth rate of China's real output per worker over the period 1980–2004 was 7.2 per cent and the predicted growth rate 6.7 per cent, a similarity which is reassuring. Comparing China with sub-Saharan Africa, the difference in predicted growth rates was 5.6 per cent. Capital accumulation accounted for no less than 54 per cent of this difference. Other contributions came from China's slower population growth, higher level of human capital, conditional convergence gain, and more dramatic sectoral change.

A second exercise provided an explanation of growth rates across China's provinces. Estimates of the contribution of total investment and its components show powerful positive effects.[4] Physical capital formation was the main explanation for the variation in provincial growth rates. The coefficient on the total investment/GDP ratio implies that a 1 percentage point rise in that ratio is associated with a 0.2 per cent higher growth rate of GDP per capita, and in the case of capital formation classified as 'innovation investment', the growth rate rises by 0.3 per cent per annum. Human capital was also found to contribute to growth at the secondary level and, especially, at the tertiary level. For instance, a 1 percentage point increase in higher education enrolment expressed as a proportion of population, when properly instrumented, leads to higher GDP per capita annual growth of 2.8 percentage points. This important contribution can be explained by the remarkable neglect of higher education, and consequent scarcity of tertiary graduates, throughout the first two decades of economic reform.

---

[3] The methodology was to apply the panel data system GMM estimator to the augmented Solow model in order to investigate causal relationships (Knight and Ding, 2012: ch.4).

[4] Cross-province panel data system GMM analysis was used to estimate informal growth regressions (Knight and Ding, 2012: ch.6).

Rapid growth has involved a great structural transformation of the economy: a closed economy became an open economy enjoying the benefits of China's comparative advantage; there was a relative expansion of the private sector and contraction of the state sector; a great transfer took place of labour from agriculture to industry, from rural to urban activities. In each case, resources were transferred from a less to a more productive sector. Knight and Ding (2012: ch. 7) examine the contribution that these three forms of structural change made to its growth rate:[5] All three prove to be important, and when their full effect on China's growth rate is combined in a single equation, they sum up to no less than 4.1 per cent of GDP per annum.

Prior to economic reform, China had an extremely closed economy. It began to move in the direction of a genuinely open economy in the 1990s: the nominal tariff was 43 per cent in 1992 and 17 per cent in 1999. The prospect of WTO membership, achieved in 2001, was a powerful motivating factor. China was now able to exploit its great comparative advantage in unskilled labour-intensive manufactures. The trade to GDP ratio was 10 per cent in 1978 but as high as 72 per cent in 2008. The estimates indicate that a 1 per cent rise in a province's growth rates of international exports or imports raises its growth rate of GDP per capita by 0.2 per cent and 0.1 per cent, respectively. More trade raises economic efficiency via the improved resource allocation, technology, and competition that openness can bring.

The distinguishing feature of China's institutional reform was the emergence of new forms of ownership, and this emergence serves as a proxy for other institutional reforms that accompanied it. Privatisation and new private firms expanded the private sector rapidly, and the greater share of private ownership in enterprise production raised productive efficiency. For instance, a 1 percentage point *fall* in the state share of (constant) industrial output raises the growth rate of GDP per capita by 0.03 per cent and a 1 percentage point *rise* in the private share raises it by 0.04 per cent. The private sector, with its incentives for profit and thus for economic efficiency, has been the institutional driving force in China's growth.

It is particularly interesting to quantify the contribution of sectoral change to the growth rate. Knight and Ding (2012) find that the effect of labour realloca-tion on growth is greater the higher is the average productivity in non-agriculture relative to agriculture, and that a 1 percentage point rise in the growth rate of the ratio of industrial output to total output in a province raises its growth rate of GDP per capita by 0.2 percentage points. Industrial growth

---

[5] The authors again use the cross-province system GMM estimator, developing the baseline equation one variable at a time (Knight and Ding, 2012: ch.7).

makes a powerful contribution to China's economic growth through improved sectoral allocation and externalities specific to industry.

2.3 The Underlying Causes

An understanding of this remarkable success requires an analysis not only of the 'proximate' determinants of economic growth outlined above but also of the 'underlying' determinants, which may be more important. Even in 1988, at the start of our study period and after the rural reforms of the early 1980s had raised rural incomes, China was still extremely poor. Although currency exchange rates can be misleading guides, in that year China's GDP per capita was only 43 per cent that of sub-Saharan Africa. It is likely that people in China were poorer on average than those in black Africa. Under central planning the economy had suffered from bad policies and lack of incentives for economic efficiency. When the economic reformers within the CCP acquired power in 1978, they recognised that it was unpopular and had lost political legitimacy, which they tried to restore through rapid economic growth and rising living standards. They embarked on a reform programme that was efficiency-enhancing and interest-compatible.

The first decade was largely one of rural reform. The de-collectivisation of the communes and restoration of household production provided incentives for effort and investment, and permitted an explosion of township, village, and private enterprises that met the demand that the urban state-owned enterprises (SOEs) had neglected. It was 'reform without losers'. The second decade involved several simultaneous urban reforms that overcame vested interests and created markets, developed a private sector, and accepted a relative decline of the state sector. After China's entry into the WTO in 2001, there was a great expansion of export-led GDP.

It is arguable that throughout the reform period the authoritarian leadership has been most concerned with the need for 'social stability', and that the most important policy to maintain social stability, and so to keep the CCP in power, was to achieve rapid economic growth, and to place this objective above all others. As the political constraints on economic reform were overcome, China gradually became a 'developmental state' (Knight, 2014). We define a developmental state as one in which government accords the highest policy priority to economic growth and adopts institutional arrangements and incentive structures which will promote that objective. In China, political control is centralised but economic management is decentralised. This creates a classic principal-agent problem. Central government aims to solve the principal-agent problem by creating incentives for officials at all levels of government to pursue its own economic objectives. These objectives have primarily been the achievement of rapid economic growth.

There have been three forms of incentives: the system of state appointments, local fiscal powers for revenue retention, and powers of patronage. There are promotion and demotion arrangements at every level of government, which determine every state official's career path. Each level of government controls personnel at the level immediately below. Evaluation has been based on performance in achieving state objectives and targets, in particular economic growth in the relevant jurisdiction. These performance criteria convert many bureaucrats into entrepreneurs. There is evidence, surveyed in Knight (2014: 1339–40), that the personnel incentive system is effective. The decentralisation of fiscal responsibility and power means that local economic development benefits local revenue and thus local government expenditure. A web of patronage enables officials to get the loyalty and support of subordinates. Patronage extends beyond the state sector because private businesses have to maintain good relationships with government and party officials. The power of patronage stems from hierarchical control – the right to grant permissions and refusals – over much of the economy.

The evidence highlights the great importance of huge capital accumulation for China's rapid economic growth. The total investment to GDP ratio was as high as 30 per cent in the early years of reform, rising to 40 per cent in recent years (Knight and Ding, 2012: Figure 1). How and why was investment so high? Such an investment rate would have been unsustainable without a matching saving rate. There are several evidence-based explanations (surveyed in Knight and Ding, 2012: 160–5) of the very high saving, one of which is the difficulty of households and private businesses to obtain credit. The rate of return on capital was initially high and rose over time, assisted by rapid total factor productivity growth and abundant cheap, disciplined labour. Entrepreneurial expectations of rapid growth were important for high investment. The developmental state was crucial. Bureaucrats were rewarded for promoting investment and private business could take investment decisions confident that growth policies would be pursued. The Chinese economy has been in a virtuous circle with sustaining feedback effects. High investment contributed to rapid economic growth, and rapid growth then produced buoyant expectations, which in turn elicited high investment.

2.4 China's Future Economic Growth

China's economic growth rate has begun to slow down, being 6.1 per cent in 2019. This reflects in part the movement towards full employment of labour and other resources. The labour force was now shrinking and labour costs were rising rapidly. It became increasingly important to improve the efficiency of resource use. The slowdown also reflects the forces of growth convergence that are evident in many countries as they develop: rapid capital accumulation began to cause diminishing returns to capital and lower expected returns to investment. Moreover, it is likely that the growing trade tensions and geopolitical competition of recent years has deterred some investment.

Higher education enrolments increased almost sixfold between 1998 and 2008 (Knight et al., 2017). This expansion and also public support for R&D, patenting, and innovation – by moving comparative advantage towards more skill- and technology-intensive products – might delay the deceleration of growth that is predicted on the basis of international experience.

The growth rate might suffer from a negative shock, for instance, a financial crash resulting from its immature financial system or a loss of investor confidence owing to social instability. The housing bubble that has emerged in recent years carries the threat of a collapse in house prices and of the heavily indebted property developers. There is evidence that happiness (i.e. subjective well-being scores) has not risen despite the rapid growth of household income per capita (Knight and Gunatilaka, 2011; Knight, Ma and Gunatilaka, 2022). and that economic growth has involved a societal cost (Knight, 2016). China's economic governance institutions can generate corruption and rent-seeking. According to the *World Governance Report* (World Bank, 2018), in 2018, among more than 200 countries China was in the 8th percentile (from the bottom) on 'voice and accountability', and in the 46th percentile on 'control of corruption'. Rapid economic growth has taken its toll of the environment. China's remarkable growth rate up to now cannot be extrapolated into the future with any confidence.

2.5 Conclusion

The empirical analyses provided results that are important for understanding China's remarkable economic growth. In particular, capital was accumulated very rapidly, and this involved great structural transformation, from a closed to an open economy, from state to private production, and from agriculture to industry. Each of these transfers meant higher productivity and thus contributed to the growth rate.

These are the proximate determinants of economic growth but the underlying determinants are also crucial. China's political economy required rapid growth in order to maintain social stability, which in turn required incentive structures at all levels of government towards that objective. This developmental state created a self-sustaining virtuous circle of economic growth.

It is interesting to contrast China's successful experience of opening up its economy with that of many other countries in the developing world, which instead experienced de-industrialisation and poor economic performance. The explanation is to be found in China's powerful comparative advantage in relatively unskilled labour-intensive products together with the other factors, listed above, that contributed to China's industrial success. This combination was generally lacking in other countries whose governments attempted to open up their economies. There are reasons why recent policies might delay the deceleration of China's growth that can be expected from international experience. However, various threats could break the virtuous circle that has maintained rapid growth up to now.

Other developing countries might wish to emulate China's economic growth success by creating a similar developmental state. They should be aware, however, that it might come at a cost to society: authoritarian governance can involve a lack of accountability with potential for socio-economic ill-effects.

3 Rural Development: From Being Farmer to Work as Wage Earner or Self-Employed

3.1 Introduction

In this section, we will look in more detail at development in rural China. The economic history from the introduction of the People's Republic in 1949 was first a story about strong influences from the Soviet Union. Private ownership of land was abolished, and user rights were handed over to its cultivators. This was followed by collectivisation and thereafter the establishment of Peoples Communes. China's development policy, at that time, created a very large division between the, by size, minority population in the cities and the majority in the rural areas. Those two categories were separated by the *hukou* system, which registered all inhabitants as either urban or rural. The development strategy of the People's Republic meant promoting growth of industries in urban areas, while the rural population had to deliver agricultural products at very low prices. (Knight and Song, 1999) Unlike urban residents, rural inhabitants had to fund their housing and health care by themselves. Rural inhabitants also had to pay fees for basic education, and they did not have access to pensions and other social insurance benefits. Thus, the urban population was prioritised at the expense of the rural population.

When the activities of the People's Communes have been positively valued, this has related to their providing rudimentary health care and basic education. However, for many observers in the West it took time to understand the scale of the mass famine and the excess mortality that plagued rural China from the end of the 1950s to the first years of the 1960s. In those years Chinese agriculture was unable to retain enough food to feed the rural population. This fact is important to understand why China's economic reforms began in the rural areas. They started after the death of Mao Zedong in 1976, and soon almost all the

People's Communes were abolished. Farmers obtained the right to cultivate land privately, but not to sell it. The reforms were followed by very rapid increases in agricultural production as farmers responded to the new incentives.

Another very important change during the first reform years was that rural people were given opportunities to look for income-rewarding activities outside agriculture. Some could find employment in the Township and Village Enterprises (TVEs) that grew rapidly. An alternative was to start small enterprises in, for example, trade, transport, or services. Other new job opportunities could be found in the cities. Stimulated by the very large wage differences, many rural people rushed to the cities. As it was (and to some extent still is) difficult to convert a residence permit (*hukou*) from rural to urban, most migrants moved back to their rural origin after a period in the cities.

The great rural to urban migration has had far-reaching consequences for the size of the rural population. In 1980, and according to official statistics, 80 per cent of China's population lived in a rural area. Owing to births and longer lives, the size of the rural population grew until 1995, when it peaked at 860 million. However, because of the large migration streams, the size of the rural population thereafter began to decrease. As consequence, in 2018 the rural population numbered 564 million and made up only 40 per cent of China's population.

Much of rural policy in China since the end of the 1980s has to be seen in the light of the policy in place during the preceding decades. Corrective measures have led to the abolition of agricultural tax and the introduction of subsidies on agricultural production. Rural households' fees for basic education have been abolished and the private costs for health care reduced. A lately introduced measure was to establish a system of social assistance (*dibao*) in China's rural areas. Such a system had been introduced in China's urban areas in the 1990s.

In this section, we will take a closer look at how China's rural areas have changed since the end of the 1980s by studying how different types of employment have changed. We will examine the proportion of people and of households that are employed as farmers, as self-employed, and as wage earners. We will discuss the characteristics and the incomes of people and households with these different kinds of employment. We will also investigate the economic benefits from changing from farming to self-employment or to wage employment, and how such gains have changed over time.

3.2 The Different Kinds of Employment

When studying rural development in China, the well-known Lewis model is a useful point of departure (Lewis, 1954; Gollin, 2014). In this framework the economy consists of two sectors: the 'modern' (capitalist) and the 'traditional' (subsistence sector). The former includes industries using capital and technology that can be of an advanced nature. Workers have different levels of qualifications, and their wages are influenced by demand and supply. The traditional sector employs farmers, handicraft workers, petty traders, and domestic servants who live near the subsistence level as supply of unqualified workers is 'unlimited'. Economic development in the Lewis framework takes place as employment in the modern sector increases at the expense of jobs in the traditional sector. We will return to the Lewis model in Section 5 looking more closely at development in urban China.

In rural China the introduction of economic reforms led to a rapid increase in wage employment and in self-employment. To transfer out of farm employment is not a random process. For example, initially the transition into self-employment was most important in the richer, more developed regions of China (Mohapatra et al., 2007). Xiao and Wu (2021), analysing 2010 data, reported that good health and longer education increased the probability of being self-employed. Among men, being married increased the probability of being self-employed. However, one should also understand that during the decades here studied agriculture became increasingly commercialised and also more productive – processes we have not studied.

In the following we will summarise the study of Gustafsson and Zhang (2022). They define three types of employed individuals among adults aged under sixty-five living in rural China: farmers, self-employed, and wage earners. Estimates of their proportions based on CHIP surveys for the years from 1988 to 2018 will be reported. Rural households in China typically have more than one adult member aged under sixty-five. As different members can have different sorts of employment, we will report estimates of employment categories at the household level. Hybrid categories are also included.

3.3 The Development of Different Kinds of Employment in Rural China

We now turn to estimates of how the proportion of rural adult individuals were employed in the CHIP survey years. Several observations can be made based on what is reported in Table 1. First, we can note that the proportion of adults employed as wage earners or in self-employment expanded between most years studied. Between 1988 and 1995 the expansion was slow. The percentage of adults working as farmers decreased only from 83 per cent to 78 per cent. More change took place between 1995 and 2002 as the proportion of farmers reduced

Table 1 Individual employment categories in rural China, 1988, 1995, 2002, 2013, and 2018, percentage

Year	Farmers	Wage earners	Self-employed	Total (rounded)	Number of observations in total
1988	83.4	14.8	1.8	100	15,399
1995	78.1	18.9	3.1	100	14,184
2002	62.3	32.4	5.3	100	11,213
2013	26.8	62.3	10.9	100	17,812
2018	25.5	62.9	11.4	100	15,933

Source: Gustafsson and Zhang (2022). Estimates based on CHIP and sample weights used.

to 62 per cent. The largest drop in the proportion of farmers happened from 2002 to 2013. In that year no more than 27 per cent of the adults were classified as farmers. Thereafter, very little change in the proportions took place.

Why had the change in employment structure come to a halt in 2013? One reason, important if possibly not the only answer, is changes in public policy. For example, the abolition of farm taxes and the introduction of agricultural subsidies and other policy reforms corresponded to an increase of farmers' income of 20–30 per cent (Naughton, 2018: 272–7).

Looking at the numbers in Table 1 in more detail, we see that each year more people were employed as wage earners than as self-employed. True, the expansion of self-employment is impressive: rising from 2 per cent of rural adults in 1988 to 12 per cent in 2018. However, between the same two years the proportion wage earners increased from 15 to 63 per cent. When disaggregating the numbers reported in Table 1 it becomes evident that the decline in farming employment was initially more pronounced in the eastern region of China. For example, in 1988, 24 per cent of adults in the eastern regions were wage earners, while the corresponding proportion in the western regions was as low as 5 per cent. Over time these regional differences became less pronounced, although differences have remained.

Shifting the focus from the individual's employment to how members of households were employed gives a supplementary picture. It becomes evident that initially very few households had specialised in wage earning or in self-employment. In 1988, only 4 per cent of all households had all their adult members employed as wage earners and only 0.6 per cent were in self-employment. However, thereafter specialisation in each of these activities increased rapidly. To mix employment within a household also became common, particularly among the self-employed. For example, while in 2013, 7 per cent of rural households had specialised in self-employment, an additional 12 per cent had at least one adult involved in such employment.

3.4 Analysing Type of Employment and the Pay-Off from Different Types of Employment

We now turn to what characterises individuals who have a high probability to belong to one of the three forms of employment, summarising the most important results in Gustafsson and Zhang (2022), where the situations in 1995 and 2018 were compared.

Rural workers in China have aged from being on average thirty-six years in 1995 to forty-four years in 2018, a year when farmers were on average fifty-two years old. Age is important for type of employment. The probability of working as a wage earner is negatively related to age while the opposite is the case for being a farmer. Among men, being married increases the probability of being self-employed and reduces that of being a wage earner, whereas the opposite is the case among married women. Those results indicate that employment decisions are taken at the household level and are influenced by prevailing gender norms.

A positive relationship between being a member in China's Communist Party and being a wage earner, and a negative relationship of CCP membership and being a farmer is found. This relationship was weaker in 2018 than in 1995. A possible interpretation is that party membership has become less important as labour market forces have become stronger. Not surprisingly, the relationship between the length of education and the probability of being a farmer is negative and the probability of being a wage earner is positive. While positive relationships between income in the county where the household lived and the probability of being wage earner as well as being self-employed were found for 1995, this was not the case in 2018. This difference indicates that a spatial convergence process had taken place in rural China across those years.

Gustafsson and Zhang (2022) also analysed income per capita among households with different forms of employment. They found that the income gap between households specialised in self-employment or wage earning and farming increased rapidly from 1988 to 1995. In 1995, the self-employed households received average incomes more than four times that of farmer households. An income function analysis showed that, although to some extent such differences could be attributed to productive characteristics, a household had strong incentives to change from farming to specialise in self-employment. Over the following years, when an increasing number of persons became wage earners or self-employed, such pay-offs decreased. However, even in 2018 a household with given characteristics could receive a higher income in self-employment or wage employment than in farming.

3.5 Conclusions

Rural China has experienced very large changes in employment during the three decades since the end of the 1980s. Among adults there has been a rapid flight from agriculture to wage employment or self-employment. These changes were particularly rapid between 2002 and 2013, when the changes were, compared also to what other countries have experienced in history, rather rapid. However, after 2013 such changes appear to have come to a halt, possibly temporarily and as response to changed policy.

People who have become wage earners are younger and more educated than those who work as farmers. Self-employment in rural China is an activity mainly for married men, not for married women. Moving from agriculture to wage employment or self-employment have led to higher income. Such income gains were highest back in 1995, when few households had made that move.

4 The Labour Market and Economic Reform: From Labour System to Labour Market

4.1 Introduction

Sections 4 and 5 are both concerned with China's labour market. This section shows how the labour system evolved to become a labour market, with important implications for both efficiency and equity. It draws on the book on this subject by Knight and Song (2005). The next section shows how the labour force, initially abundant, eventually became scarce, with important implications for people's incomes and for society.

To ensure the efficient and equitable use of China's labour force, how should the society and economy be organised; in particular, what role should a labour market play? At the start of our period of study the administered labour system remained largely intact in urban China, and restrictions on labour remained pervasive in rural China. The remarkable growth and transformation of the economy – involving the creation of new product and factor markets and 'the greatest migration in human history' – has necessitated vast and rapid change in the allocation, use, and remuneration of labour. The accompanying labour market reform has affected the quality of life of hundreds of millions of people.

4.2 The Labour System

Under central planning China was compartmentalised into an 'invisible Great Wall' between rural and urban areas. There was, and to some extent still is, a rigid system of household registration (*hukou*), which accorded different rights and duties to urban and rural people, to the disadvantage of the latter. Despite it having been a peasant-led revolution, there was a large rural–urban divide in incomes and in many spheres of life, as analysed in the earlier book by Knight and Song (1999). The disbanding of the communes in the first half of the 1980s and the restoration of incentives raised peasant incomes but, as urban reforms advanced, the ratio of urban to rural household income per capita grew, and it reached a peak of 3.32 in 2009. This reflects in part the unbalanced nature of political influence, however latent it might have been (Knight et al., 2006).

Rural–urban migration was outside the labour system. It was limited at the start of our study period but began to grow in the 1990s and became a flood in the 2000s. It took a particular form, reflecting tenurial institutions and government policy. In principle, the large gap between urban and rural income per capita provides a great incentive for migration, and there was apparently no shortage of would-be migrants. However, the Chinese government has controlled and curbed the inflow of migrants into the cities and towns, partly to protect urban people against labour market competition and partly to avoid the ills of excessive migration that are evident in parts of the developing world. Rural–urban migrant inflows have been regulated to meet the urban demand for migrant labour, and migrants have been allowed into the cities only on a temporary basis. Urban settlement of rural–urban migrants and conferment of the rights of urban people are made very difficult, although changes have taken place in recent years, especially in the smaller and medium-sized cities.

4.3 The Evolving Wage Structure

China evolved gradually from having a centrally planned urban labour system towards having a flexible urban labour market (Knight and Song, 2005). As a labour market develops, so we expect wage levels more closely to reflect the forces of demand and supply and wage structure more closely to reflect the productivity of labour and the efficiency of its use. How did China's urban wage structure evolve? It is possible to examine changes in the wage structure drawing on the CHIP surveys, as analysed in Knight and Song (2005) for 1988–95, Knight and Song (2008) for 1995–2002, and Gustafsson and Wan (2020) for 2002–7 and 2007–13.

In the late 1980s most urban workers were employed in SOEs, and these 'work units' provided them with mini-welfare states. Urban *hukou* labour was allocated bureaucratically and movement from one work unit to another was extremely rare, wages were administered according to a national pay scale, and the wage structure was highly egalitarian. It was said the 'brain workers' were paid less than 'hand workers'. The period 1988–95 witnessed some decentralisation in decision-making in labour matters. Government and its SOE agents were willing to trade off some wage equality for more efficiency through the provision of incentives.

Wage inequality rose sharply: the Gini coefficient of urban wages increased from an extremely low level of 0.23 in 1988 to 0.31 in 1995. The median real wage rose by as much as 6 per cent per annum. Wage function analysis showed the rewards for human capital increasing from very low levels: the returns to education and the returns to occupation-based skills both rose. The initial upwards shape of the age-earnings profile – reflecting institutionalised payments for seniority – became more bowed, in line with human capital theory. However, there was also evidence of emerging wage discrimination against women (further discussed in Section 9) and for Communist Party (CPC) members. Segmentation grew between the wages of the expanding private sector and the, less competitive, state sector.

The pace of labour market reform quickened over the subsequent seven years, 1995–2002. The state no longer took responsibility for matching the demand and supply of urban labour, and employers increasingly determined the wages of their employees. Wages became more open to market forces. However, this process was experienced very unevenly.

In the late 1990s, government was forced by increased loss-making and the consequent fiscal costs to retrench urban workers from the SOEs. Many millions of workers in urban China lost their jobs, and open unemployment became a major problem for the first time. The true rate of urban unemployment rose from 4.2 per cent in 1990 to 11.5 per cent in 2000 (Knight and Song, 2005: 35). The urban *hukou* employees who were retrenched (11.4 per cent of the total) experienced long durations of unemployment, and many faced a tough competitive informal labour market and lower re-employment wages, despite the fact that city governments, trying to protect their residents, responded by curbing the employment of migrants (Appleton et al., 2002). After the bloated public-owned sector was deflated, economic efficiency improved and net rural–urban migration grew once again.

The retrenchment programme might be thought of as a controlled experiment, creating a labour market overnight. However, those urban workers who were not laid off maintained their higher wages, being relatively protected from competition. The Gini coefficient of urban wages increased from 0.31 to 0.37, partly because of this new segmentation. Urban *hukou* real wage growth averaged 7 per cent per annum over the seven years but unskilled wages lagged well behind. The earlier pattern of change in wage structure continued. Human capital was increasingly rewarded. For instance, over the fourteen years from 1988, the premium of college education over primary education rose from 8 per cent to 88 per cent. Whereas in 1995 the age-wage profile was sharply bowed because it was the younger and the older age groups who encountered the strongest competition, by 2002 it took the normal market shape because there was now more competition across the age range. There was a high degree of wage segmentation across ownership types and across provinces. Decomposition analysis showed that in both periods the greatest contributions to the increase in mean real wages were made by the human capital and the province variables.

Analysis of the 2002, 2007, and 2013 urban surveys by Gustafsson and Wan (2020) revealed a Gini coefficient of wage inequality rising from 0.35 to 0.38 but then remaining at 0.38. One reason for the recent stability of wage inequality is the behaviour of the coefficient on years of schooling. This fell from 0.102 to 0.068 between 2007 and 2013. That fall is likely to be the result of the remarkable, almost sixfold, expansion of higher education between 1990 and 2008, with a consequent fall in the returns to college education after 2007 (Knight, Li and Deng 2017). Nevertheless, years of schooling still contributed about half of wage inequality in 2013. Years of experience continued to be well rewarded: twenty years of experience can be estimated to raise the wage by 80 per cent. Communist Party membership received a wage premium, as also did being male: its coefficient rose from 0.19 to 0.28 over the eleven years.[6] State firms and foreign-owned firms continued to be the best-paying ownership types.

4.4 Labour Market Segmentation

How can the continuing labour market imperfections be explained? Perhaps it was the lack of wage discrimination in 1988 that was the outlier. Wage differences, for instance by gender or by affiliation, are found in many market economies, not only in urban China. However, we could not distinguish between the pure discrimination effect and the effect of related but unobserved characteristics such as ability; in fact, few studies manage to do so.

---

[6] We will return to the issue of how the wage gap between female and male workers changed in Section 9.

Some of the observed wage segmentation is specific to China. Differences in the pace of reform created spatial segmentation of wages but controls on movement prevented it from being curtailed by equilibrating immobility of labour. Mobility of workers from one firm to another constrained the creation of a labour market. Even in 1999, the average duration of an urban *hukou* employee's completed job was twenty years, and 78 per cent of them were still in their first job. Job stickiness begets wage stickiness. Until the new millennium urban workers' job mobility was low and wage differences across firms were not ironed out by labour market competition.

Knight and Li (2005) provided a partial explanation for the conditional wage differences by ownership type. They analysed the effect of enterprise profitability on wages in China's formal sector. Standardising for individual worker characteristics, firm profitability was found to raise wages substantially. In the close-knit Chinese *danwei* there are reasons why a failure to share profits can lead to the tacit withdrawal of cooperation by workers. Thus, there was evidence of profit-sharing, the likely explanation for which was this form of efficiency wage behaviour.

There is one sort of labour segmentation that cannot be captured by our older data sets because they cover only urban residents with urban *hukous*. Rural–urban migrants, with rural *hukous*, were for many years at a great and discriminatory disadvantage in the urban labour market; there is conflicting evidence as to whether it is still common. They had to take the least attractive jobs – the jobs that urban-born people did not want. Their wages were lower, more likely being the result of market forces than of institutional factors. They had fewer of the rights that urban-born workers possessed, such as rights to pensions, to health insurance and unemployment insurance, and so on (Knight and Song, 2005). Many migrants returned home permanently after an urban spell, and those who kept coming back retained close links with their rural households. Permanent urban settlement has encountered serious obstacles, especially in the largest cities, although the degree of segmentation has gradually weakened over time.

Another form of wage segmentation was that between the informal and the formal sector. In the former, wages were set competitively, while in the latter, wages were higher – for institutional or efficiency reasons – than the competitive level would have been. Liang et al. (2016) treated possession of a formal contract of employment as the criterion for formality, reflecting sharp differences in wage benefits and non-wage benefits. On that basis, according to the CHIP survey of 2013, formal employees were 43 per cent of total urban employment and informal workers 57 per cent, the latter being divided between informal employees (42 per cent) and business owners (15 per cent). Most rural *hukou* workers were informally employed. The rapid growth of urban employment and particularly of rural–urban migrants meant that a larger proportion of the urban labour market became competitive and informal, so making more wages responsive to the forces of demand and supply.

4.5 Conclusion

By comparison with China's rural reform, urban reform was slow and gradual, well described by the saying 'crossing the river by feeling the stones'. There were two main obstacles to progress. One was the vested interests of SOEs and their privileged urban workers. The other was the need for coordination of various interacting reforms – for instance enterprise, housing, and financial reform – giving rise to problems of sequencing. Both obstacles were relevant to the slow pace – over thirty years – of moving from a labour system to a labour market.

There is a good deal of evidence for the main hypothesis that an urban labour market has emerged, and that its wage structure has evolved to reflect the productivity of labour. The process was slowed by the need for other reforms. For instance, some constraints on the mobility of labour were lifted only in the new millennium, and some remain in the largest cities. The urban labour market remains seriously segmented in policy-related ways: China is still moving towards a competitive labour market.

This section's contribution has been to provide a fascinating account of how, over thirty years, an important country – gradually, without a clear road map, solving problems along the way, avoiding a big bang, and probably uniquely in the world – started from the shackles of an inflexible labour system and moved a long way towards the formation of a functioning labour market.

5 The Labour Market and Migration: From Labour Surplus to Labour Scarcity

5.1 Introduction

Throughout the twentieth century China was a surplus labour economy par excellence. Even at the time of liberation – mid-century – almost all of the arable land was in use, and in the next half century the rural population and labour force more than doubled. In the 1980s, the increase was absorbed mainly by rural industrialisation outside the planning system, but as urban reforms progressed the main absorption of the growing rural labour force was through rural–urban migration.

The remarkable growth of the Chinese economy – averaging 10 per cent per annum over the reform period, and in particular the growth of the urban economy – required a great inflow of labour into the cities and towns. This need was accentuated by the slow growth of the urban-born labour force. The draconian one-child family policy, introduced in the late 1970s, began to slow down the growth of the urban-born labour force in the 2000s; its effect had been delayed by Mao's baby boom of the 1960s and 1970s and its echo when the baby boomers reached reproductive age. The number of rural–urban migrant workers in China is now rather large. The phenomenon has been referred to as 'the greatest migration in human history'.

Lewis (1954), the article introduced in Section 3, on 'economic development with unlimited supplies of labour' may well be the most famous and the most cited article in development economics. It presents a model of a dual economy in which economic growth occurs through the transfer of labour from the, less productive, traditional sector to the, more productive, modern sector. In the initial, 'classical' stage, traditional sector labour is freely available to the modern sector at a constant wage. As economic development proceeds, traditional sector labour becomes scarce and its supply curve to the modern sector becomes upwards-sloping, and increasingly steeply so. This is the 'neoclassical' stage, in which the benefits of economic development become more widely shared, including rural people who migrate and those who remain. Between the two stages is a turning point.

The Lewis model has huge implications for the alleviation of poverty and the reduction of inequality. Entry to the second stage might be the most important market mechanism for tackling income inequality in a developing country. Therefore, it is an important question: has China passed the turning point and entered the second stage of the Lewis model? We draw on Knight (2021).

5.2 The Great Migration

Table 2 covers the period 1990–2020. Before that time rural–urban migration was heavily constrained. The table records that the number of rural *hukou* workers in the urban areas increased from 42 million (25 per cent of urban formal employment) in 1995 to 257 million in 2015 (64 per cent of urban formal employment), and by extrapolation 320 million (70 per cent) in 2020. Migrants as a proportion of the rural-born labour force increased from 8 per cent in 1990 to 20 per cent in 2005, and to 41 per cent in 2015. A slightly different picture emerges from NBS direct estimates of rural *hukou* people working in towns and cities derived from representative rural surveys ('directly measured', not 'as a residual').[7] The survey figure exceeded the residual figure by 24 million in 2000 and by 47 million in 2010 but fell short of it in 2020 (extrapolated from 2018) by 26 million. The number of rural–urban migrants grew most rapidly in the period 2005–10, when the growth of real GDP was particularly rapid, averaging over 11 per cent per annum. The slower increase in surveyed migrants

---

[7] NBS, Monitoring Survey Report on Off-farm Workers, annual (in Chinese).

Table 2 Chinese trends in urban employment, urban-born labour force, rural–urban migration, and rural resident labour force (million)

	1990	1995	2000	2005	2010	2015	2020
Urban employment	170	190	232	273	346	404	459
Urban-born labour force	128	136	143	148	151	147	139
Rural–urban migrants: directly measured	n.a.	67	113	126	242	277	294
as residual as % of urban	42	54	89	125	195	257	320
Employment residual as % of rural-born	25	28	38	46	56	64	70
Labour force	8	10	15	20	31	41	51
Rural-born labour force	519	544	578	610	663	666	654
Rural resident labour force	477	490	489	485	468	409	334

Sources: Knight and Song (2005), figure 10.1; Knight et al. (2011), table 10; *China Statistical Yearbook*, various issues; NBS, Monitoring Survey Report on Off-farm Workers, annual (in Chinese).

Notes: The baseline for the projections is provided by the official 1 per cent Population Survey of 2005. It contains detailed information for cities, towns, and rural areas on population by age, on age-specific mortality rates, and on age-specific labour force participation rates. The number of entries to and retirements from the urban-born labour force are estimated in each year from 2005 onwards; people are assumed to enter at age eighteen and to retire at age sixty. The five-year age-specific mortality rates in 2004 are used to estimate annual deaths in each age group. The age-specific participation rates of 2005 are used to convert the population of working age to labour force. The figure for directly measured rural–urban migrants in 2020 (294 million) is extrapolated from 2018 (286 million).

after 2010 can be attributed to the drastic contraction of the age group twenty to twenty-nine in rural China, structural change towards skill- and technology-intensive activities for which many rural workers were ill-prepared, and the deceleration of economic growth.

However, the choice of migrant measure does not affect the basic story that migrant numbers have continued to increase in the face of the static urban-born labour force. With the exception of college graduates or those coming from the armed forces – who are given urban *hukous* – rural *hukou* migrants have been absorbed into the urban labour market partly by entering newly created jobs and partly by moving to jobs that urban-born workers no longer occupied.

5.3 The Lewis Turning Point

In about 2010 there were signs that China's traditional labour surplus was drying up and that scarcity of rural–urban migrant labour – at existing wages – had begun to appear in at least some parts of China. An inconclusive literature on the Lewis turning point emerged. The most significant contribution was made in a special issue on this topic in *China Economic Review* in 2011. The different authors did not agree on whether China had reached the turning point of the Lewis model. This is not surprising because of their different methodologies and data sets and because a turning stage rather than a single point is to be expected in such a large and diverse country characterised by poorly integrated labour markets. In their contribution Knight et al. (2011), using national data, found that migrant real wages began to rise more rapidly at about that time. However, they also adduced evidence that a substantial rural labour surplus remained. The authors attributed this apparent inconsistency to institutional and other restrictions which held back the remaining supply of the rural labour force. The passage of time would be needed to answer the question being posed. A decade later the topic now attracts less attention, essentially because there is more agreement that scarcity of unskilled labour has indeed become a general phenomenon.

When the supply of labour is in abundance, the market wage of relatively unskilled labour is held down by competitive forces. One test of whether an economy moves from the first to the second stage of the Lewis model is to be found in the behaviour of unskilled market wages, in particular the wages of rural–urban migrants. Table 3 shows how the migrant real wage increased over the period 2000–18. It implies that migrant real wages grew over the periods 2002–07 by 8.0 per cent per annum, 2007–13 by as much as 12.0 per cent per annum, and 2013–18 by 6.3 per cent per annum. These results are consistent with China entering the second stage of the Lewis model in the period 2007–13, when the increase in rural–urban migration was at its peak, but the deceleration of real wage growth in the next five years is unexpected.

Interpretation is complicated by the existence of and changes in minimum wage legislation. Minimum wages are likely to be important for rural–urban migrants, being normally at the bottom of the urban wage distribution. In principle, minimum wage policies can serve two purposes. One is to protect the immobile and the weak against exploitation in a labour market governed by market forces. In that case, minimum wage increases are an endogenous policy response to broader wage increases generated by market forces. The other purpose is to raise wages at the bottom of the wage distribution above the

Table 3 Chinese rural–urban migrant average real wage per month; urban and rural household real income per capita per annum; and their ratio, household income per capita Gini coefficient, 2000–18

	2000	2002	2005	2007	2010	2013	2015	2018
Migrant real wage p.c.: yuan per month	749	776	986	1,143	1,690	2,253	2,669	3,053
Annual percentage change		1.8	8.3	5.1	13.9	11.7	6.5	4.6
Urban real income p.c.:	7,585	9,337	12,019	14,785	19,109	23,866	26,415	32,199
Annual percentage change	11.0	8.8	10.	8.9	7.7	5.2	6.8	
Rural real income p.c.:	2,910	3,178	3,834	4,559	5,919	8,464	9,941	12,078
Annual percentage change		4.5	6.4	9.0	9.1	2.7	8.4	6.7
Urban/rural income p.c.:	2.61	2.94	3.14	3.24	3.23	2.82	2.66	2.66
National Gini coefficient	0.438	0.450	0.485	0.484	0.481	0.473	0.462	0.471

Sources: *China Statistical Yearbook*, various issues; NBS (online).

Notes: The migrant real wage is calculated using the urban consumer price index, and is shown at 2010 constant prices. The urban and rural real income per capita are calculated using the urban and rural consumer price indexes, respectively, and are shown at 2010 constant prices.

levels that would be determined by market forces. In that case, exogenous minimum wage policy provides an alternative explanation for the rising wages of migrants.

Provinces were required to set minimum wages for their cities and counties, and these became important in the first decade of the new century. They appeared to increase most rapidly in real terms, by 7 per cent per annum between 2004 and 2009 and by 10 per cent per annum between 2009 and 2012, after the Chinese government demanded tougher enforcement (Fang and Lin, 2020). Thereafter, the government became concerned about the burden of higher wage costs on enterprises (Deng, 2017) and no longer set minimum wage target increases. Ye et al. (2020), using the 2013 CHIP urban survey, found that 13 per cent of employees earned less than the hourly minimum wage, and that the average shortfall below it was substantial for young and less educated workers. It had been possible for employers to increase the hours of work that were required in response to increases in the monthly minimum wage. These policies and this evidence cast doubt on a market interpretation of rapid migrant real wage growth in the 2003–12 period but might help to explain the slower growth after 2013. Migrant real wage behaviour does not provide a conclusive test of entry into the second stage of the Lewis mechanism.

What effect can the arrival of rural labour scarcity have on the urban–rural income ratio?. On the one hand, it should drive up unskilled market wages in the cities. On the other hand, the reduced availability of labour in rural areas relative to the availability of land and other resources should raise rural labour incomes. Therefore, the ratio might either fall or rise. However, the fact that only part of the urban labour force is affected whereas the effect on rural households is likely to be widespread tips the balance towards a fall in the ratio. Moreover, if migrants (increasing in number) remit part of their (now higher) wages to their rural households, that also should reduce the urban–rural income ratio.

The ratio of urban household income per capita to rural household income per capita, having risen since the mid-1980s, peaked at 3.32 in 2009 and began to fall almost monotonically thereafter; it was down to 2.66 in 2017. The national Gini coefficient of income per capita, having risen for many years, peaked at 0.490, and fell monotonically to 4.62 in 2015. Thus, not only did the urban–rural household income ratio fall but also the national Gini coefficient of household income per capita, as Table 2 shows. This relationship is likely to be causal because of the great importance of the urban–rural income ratio for the Gini in the Chinese case. In 2007, for instance, according to the CHIP survey of that year, the ratio of urban to rural household income per capita was 4.10 (using a broader definition of income). The urban Gini was 0.34 and the rural

Gini was 0.36, whereas the national Gini, reflecting the wider income distribution, was no less than 0.49. It is through narrowing the urban–rural income gap that the Lewis mechanism can reduce the national Gini coefficient.

Other forces tend to raise the Gini coefficient. For instance, both the urban and the rural Ginis of household income per capita continued to rise as the national Gini fell. That might explain why the Gini edged upwards a little after 2015. The rise in the urban Gini is likely to reflect increasing possession of, or returns to, other factors of production, such as human and physical capital.

It is an important question, therefore, as to whether the scarcity of migrant labour, which emerged in about 2010, precipitated the decline in the urban–rural income per capita ratio, which began to fall consistently for a time after 2010. The implication would be that the arrival of labour scarcity was a powerful market mechanism for reducing income inequality.

The CHIP surveys report that household real income per capita in rural areas doubled over the years 2007–13, increasing by 13 per cent per annum. Wage income was the most important component of that growth, accounting for 35 per cent of the increase in rural income per capita and growing by 12 per cent per annum. Non-agricultural income grew by 13 per cent per annum and net transfer income (including migrant remittances) by as much as 29 per cent per annum. Each of these rapid increases might have resulted from a growing scarcity of rural labour insofar as it improved the ratio of rural resources to rural labour and the opportunity cost of migration. This evidence for the period from 2007 onwards is consistent with growing scarcity of unskilled labour.

Nevertheless, as with the rise in minimum wages, the strengthening of government fiscal policies against rural poverty complicates the story. Social benefits as a proportion of the final income of rural households increased from 0.7 per cent in 2002 to 6.4 per cent in 2013 owing to the expansion of pensions and minimum income guarantees, known as *dibao* (Gao et al., 2019, using CHIP data). Hoken and Sato (2019), also analysing CHIP, show that rural net transfer payments to rural households from public and private sources combined grew from –4.0 per cent of final income in 2002 to 7.7 per cent in 2013. Much of the increase in private transfers represented migrant remittances. These could reflect the tightening of the labour market but public transfers would not.

5.4 Conclusion

We have documented the remarkable transfer of labour from the rural areas to the urban areas of China over a period of thirty years. For twenty of those years, this occurred while the ratio of urban to rural income per capita consistently increased. This rise was in turn an important reason for the increase in the national Gini coefficient of income inequality that we have observed. However, the ratio fell in the third decade, and national income inequality stopped rising and might have fallen a little.

Was this fall of the Gini the Lewis model in action? We have adduced evidence that the turning point was reached in the year 2010 or thereabouts. Although the evidence is consistent with our interpretation, we could not discount a role for minimum wages and for fiscal transfers. Entry to the second stage of the Lewis model cannot in any case be long delayed and will be a powerful market mechanism for reducing income inequality in future years. We will return to the issue of how income inequality in China as a whole has evolved in Section 7.

It is interesting to contrast China's experience of rural–urban migration with that of comparable countries. Although China's migration has been called 'the greatest migration in human history', its extent and its form were nevertheless restricted by government. China's inflows did not produce the vast slums in and around cities that are observable in many developing countries. The experience of slower growing economies reflects both their limited growth of urban formal sector employment opportunities and their unlimited migration into the cities. In China, by contrast, many new urban jobs were created as the urban economy grew rapidly, by well over 10 per cent per annum, and central and local governments were able to match the migrant inflows to the growing demands for labour. Both private and public enterprises had profit incentives to expand production: China possessed the comparative advantage to become 'the work-shop of the world'.

6 Public Revenues, Expenditures, and Inequality

6.1 Introduction

Public transfers that households receive through social security schemes provide a safety net for people's livelihood and help to ensure social fairness and stability in China. A major reason for low inequality in the developed countries, as revealed by international experience, lies in the government redistribution policies (Cai and Yue, 2016). Research on developed and developing countries has indicated that government transfers and personal income taxation can lower income inequality. However, as a major component of government public expenditures, social security expenditures play a more crucial role in narrowing income inequality. Their redistributive effect is much greater than that of the personal income tax (Milanovic, 2000; Mahler and Jesuit, 2006; Kristjánsson, 2011).

In Section 6, we analsze how the distribution of income is altered by public expenditures and revenues. Here we mainly focus on social security transfers and the personal income tax. We attempt to answer and explain the question: is inequality of post-transfer/tax income narrower than that of pre-transfer/tax income?

6.2 A Brief Introduction to Public Revenue and Expenditure Redistributive Polices in China

Although China has a multitiered government, in this section we take the approach of aggregating the public sectors into one entity and evaluate the joint redistributive effects of social security expenditures and personal income tax from both the central and local governments. Chinese households receive public transfers from governments mainly through a variety of social security programmes, of which the principal element is pension insurance.

Pension schemes in China include Pensions for Civil Servants and Public Sector Units (PSUs), the Employee Social Insurance Pension System, and the Urban and Rural Residents Social Pension Scheme (URSPS).[8] The targeted population of the Employee Social Insurance Pension Scheme is limited to those who worked for enterprises. Self-employed, irregular-working and non-working residents in urban and rural areas were included in the URSPS. In some sense, the enterprise worker pension and the pension scheme for civil servants and PSU workers are pension schemes for employees working in the formal sectors, whereas the urban and rural resident pension insurance is designed for those working in the informal sector (World Bank and Development Research Center of the State Council of the People's Republic of China, 2013). The three pension schemes have been established in an attempt to cover the entire population of present China.

Besides pension, medical insurance is also an important social insurance programme in China. It reimburses medical expenses actually incurred by households, which include spending in hospitalisation and outpatient services. Participants in the Urban Employee Basic Medical Insurance include employees in either the public sector or the private sector in the urban areas. Residents who do not work or work in informal sectors are covered by the Urban and Rural Residents Basic Medical Insurance system. By the end of 2020, China's basic medical insurance covered 1.36 billion people and the number of pension insurance participants reached 1 billion. China has thus by now established the world's largest social security safety net. However, it should be noted that during much of the period covered here most older rural people were not receiving any pension and rural people had to pay for their health care by

---

[8] For a fuller account of the pension system in China, see, for example, Dorfman et al. (2013).

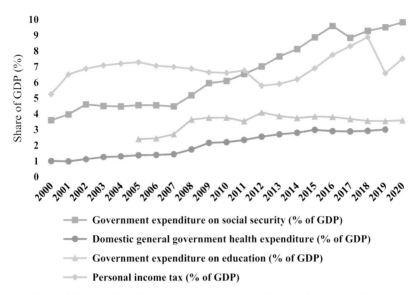

Figure 1 Trends in public revenues and expenditures (per cent of GDP)

Sources: Ministry of Finance of People's Republic of China, National Government Final Accounts, annual; NBS, China Statistical Yearbook, various issues; The World Bank data: https://data.worldbank.org/.

themselves. Most probably it is still common for elderly in rural areas to not seek medical treatment for their illnesses. In addition, the rate of reimbursement for the New Rural Cooperative Medical Insurance is lower than its counterpart in urban areas, see Feng et al., 2015.

Large-scale expenditure programmes in China involve social security, health care, and education. Figure 1 shows the trends in the shares of GDP of government expenditures on social security, health care and education, as well as the personal income tax. The Chinese government has expanded the expenditures on social security and public health care in recent years, with the share of GDP increasing almost every year. The share of the personal income tax in GDP has remained between 6 per cent and 9 per cent since 2000, which is relatively low in international comparisons. This is due to several adjustments in China's personal income tax expense deduction standards and in the tax rate structures since 2006, which have reduced the average effective rate of personal income tax as well as its share in total public revenues (Zhang, Yue, and Shao, 2020).

6.3 The Redistributive Effect of Public Expenditures and Revenues

This section uses data from five rounds of CHIP surveys from 1988 to 2018 to analsze the long-term redistributive effect of public revenues and social security transfers in China, measured by the progressivity index, redistributive effect index, and its decomposition. We will see that, thanks to the gradual expansion of the policy coverage in rural areas and the increase of its benefit level, the progressivity and the redistributive effect of the social security policies increased over years.

Redistributive effect index, which equals to the Gini coefficient of pre-transfer income C_x minus the Gini coefficient of post-transfer income C_y in equation (1), is calculated to evaluate the redistributive effects of public transfers and taxes. In the analysis of social security transfers, if the redistributive effect is positive, it indicates that the Gini coefficient of post-transfer income is smaller than the Gini coefficient of pre-transfer income. Thus, income inequality is reduced after social security transfers. Conversely, a negative redistributive means that the transfer has increased the income gap, and a score of zero implies that the transfer is neutral.

$$\text{Redistributive effect index} = G_X - G_Y = \left(C_Y^X - G_Y\right) - \frac{t}{1+t}\left(C_S^X - G_X\right)$$

$$= H + V. \tag{1}$$

To analyse the determinants of the redistributive effect index, Kakwani (1977, 1984) further decomposed the redistributive effect index into horizontal equity and vertical equity, as shown in equation (1). Horizontal equity H equals to $C_Y^X - G_Y$, where C_Y^X is the concentration ratio of post-transfer income Y ranked by pre-transfer income X. Essentially, horizontal equity is a principle of 'equal treatment of equals', which means persons who are equally well-off should be liable for the same tax or receive the same transfer. This norm thus requires that rankings of all persons should not be altered during the redistributive process. Plotnick (1981) illustrated that the value of horizonal equality H can only be zero or negative. If the transfer does not change the recipients' income ranking, the horizontal equity H will be zero. If the transfer changes the recipients' income ranking, the horizontal equity H will be negative and thus has an disequalising redistributive effect.

Vertical equity is concerned with the appropriate difference in tax or transfer treatment for persons with different levels of well-being. In the formula, vertical equity V equals to $-\frac{t}{1+t}(C_S^X - G_X)$, where t represents the average transfer rate, that is the ratio of average per capita transfer income to average per capita pre-transfer income. C_S^X is the concentration ratio of a social security transfer ranked by the pre-transfer income X. $C_S^X - G_X$ can be defined as the progressivity index P. A positive progressivity index suggests that social security transfers are more concentrated on the high-income groups and thus are regressive.

A negative P indicates that the transfers are more concentrated on the low-income groups and thus are progressive. Thus, progressive social security transfers will lead to positive vertical equity V, and thus tend to reduce income inequality. The opposite is true for the analysis on the personal income tax.

Column 4 in Table 4 shows that the progressivity indexes are negative for the nation, and the urban and rural areas each year, which means that the social security transfer concentrates more on the low-income people than the high-income groups before transfer. The redistributive effects indexes are positive almost every year for the entire country and urban and rural population groups. At the national level, the social security transfer reduced the redistributive effects index from 1995 to 2018. For example, the pre-transfer Gini coefficient in 2018 is 0.509, which is higher than that of post-transfer income (0.446), indicating that the post-transfer income gap is narrowed by 14 per cent compared to the pre-transfer period. Moreover, the redistributive effects indexes are continuously increasing from 1988 to 2018, implying that the positive redistributive effects of social security transfers have been enhanced over the past thirty years. Social security transfers reduce income inequality within urban and rural areas, and the redistributive effects are much stronger in urban than in rural. It is worth noting that the rural redistributive effects index was only 0.004 in 1988 but increased to 0.016 in 2018, indicating that the social security transfers played an increasingly important role in rural areas, especially after 2002, at the time when China started to establish a comprehensive rural social safety net.

The redistributive effects index is decomposed into two components: horizontal equity and vertical equity. The evolution of the vertical equity depends on the progressivity of the social security transfer. As the government implemented a progressive transfer initially – that is the transfers were more concentrated on low-income groups (here the income did not include the transfer) – the vertical equity went up along with the increase in the transfer rate, indicating that the equalising effect of social security transfers improved. On the other hand, horizontal equity depends on whether the distribution of the transfer is consistent with that of the pre-transfer income. When the transfer volume was small, people's income ranking was not changed by the transfer; thus, the horizontal equity was zero, and the vertical equity dominated the total redistributive effects. The transfer increase therefore decreased inequality. However, if the government increased the transfer volume without changing its distribution, the transfer recipients would gradually become a relatively high-income group after transfer. The transfer would change the income ranking and would concentrate more on the high-income people. The horizontal equity effect would be negative and surpass the vertical equity effect and increase post-transfer income inequality (Cai and Xu, 2022).

Table 4 Redistributive effects of public social security transfers

Year	Concentration ratio (1)	Pre-transfer Gini coefficient (2)	Post-transfer Gini coefficient (3)	Progressivity index (4) = (1) − (2)	Redistributive effects index (5) = (2) − (3) = (6) + (7)	Horizontal equity (6)	Vertical equity (7)
National							
1988	0.089	0.359	0.360	−0.270	−0.001	−0.024	0.023
1995	−0.145	0.442	0.432	−0.587	0.010	−0.047	0.057
2002	−0.070	0.458	0.450	−0.527	0.008	−0.051	0.059
2007	−0.137	0.523	0.487	−0.660	0.036	−0.055	0.091
2013	−0.343	0.488	0.437	−0.831	0.051	−0.084	0.135
2018	−0.387	0.509	0.446	−0.896	0.063	−0.077	0.140
Rural							
1988	0.080	0.352	0.347	−0.272	0.004	−0.003	0.007
1995	0.162	0.433	0.431	−0.271	0.002	−0.003	0.005
2002	0.161	0.381	0.384	−0.221	−0.003	−0.006	0.004
2013	0.016	0.384	0.376	−0.368	0.008	−0.012	0.019
2018	−0.066	0.419	0.403	−0.485	0.016	−0.019	0.035

Table 4 (cont.)

Year	Concentration ratio (1)	Pre-transfer Gini coefficient (2)	Post-transfer Gini coefficient (3)	Progressivity index (4) = (1) − (2)	Redistributive effects index (5) = (2) − (3) = (6) + (7)	Horizontal equity (6)	Vertical equity (7)
Urban							
1988	−0.160	0.443	0.417	−0.603	0.025	−0.035	0.060
1995	−0.254	0.273	0.224	−0.527	0.049	−0.040	0.089
2002	−0.433	0.352	0.280	−0.785	0.072	−0.069	0.141
2007	−0.361	0.391	0.334	−0.753	0.057	−0.063	0.120
2013	−0.409	0.405	0.329	−0.814	0.076	−0.048	0.123
2018	−0.465	0.445	0.356	−0.910	0.089	−0.082	0.172

Source: Calculated by the authors based on data collected in the Chinese Household Income Project (CHIP) 1988, 1995, 2002, 2007, 2013, and 2018 surveys.

Table 5 Redistributive effects of personal income tax among urban residents

Year	Average income per capita (Yuan)	Progressivity index	Average effective tax rates	Redistributive effects index
2002	7,776	0.312	0.021	0.006
2007	15,386	0.412	0.033	0.014
2013	18,931	0.421	0.030	0.013
2018	37,353	0.479	0.014	0.007

Source: Yue and Zhang (2021). Calculated from Chinese Household Income Project (CHIP) 2002, 2007, 2013, and 2018 surveys.

Note: Estimates in this table reflect the impact of the personal income tax on the income distribution of urban residents, without considering the impact on the income distribution of rural residents. Average income per capita are based on current year prices.

There are several reasons for the increased vertical equity effect of public transfers in China. For one thing, China accelerated the establishment of a comprehensive social security network in the 2000s, which covered more and more residents, especially in rural areas. After the establishment of the New Rural Pension Scheme in 2009 and the Urban Residents Pension Scheme in 2011, low-income rural and urban residents without a job are included in the social security system. The main components of the social security system have been improved and the number of beneficiaries increased dramatically. For another thing, according to the trends in progressivity indexes from 1988 to 2018, public social security expenditures are allocated more to the low-income groups, and this 'pro-poor' characteristic is gradually enhancing. Therefore, the public social security transfers have been playing an increasingly important role in China in recent years.

Table 5 reports the redistributive effect of China's personal income tax among urban residents for 2002, 2007, 2013, and 2018. Results show that although the progressivity index of the personal income tax has been increasing, the average effective tax rate decreased significantly between 2013 and 2018, and thus the income redistributive effects of the personal income tax fell. Although the personal income tax is concentrated more to the high-income groups, as the average effective tax rate was low. The personal income tax still does not play a significant role in reducing income inequality in China.

6.4 Conclusions

The redistributive effects of social security transfers in China were increasing from 1988 to 2018, at the national level as well as within urban and rural areas. It implies that the social security system has come to play a more equalising role on the income distribution over a period of thirty years. Initially the targeted population of the social security scheme was limited mainly to those who worked for enterprises in urban areas. The systems were rather different for urban and rural residents, with the latter having very limited access to social security programmes.

Several changes have been made to harmonise the systems since the beginning of the twenty-first century. Particularly the improvement of the rural social safety network has to be mentioned. The involvement of self-employed, irregular-working, or non-working rural residents in the social welfare scheme has increased. However, differences in benefit levels between rural and urban areas still remain. In should be understood that in contemporary China, the family plays a larger role for income security than in many contemporary high-income countries. The redistributive effect of the personal income tax is smaller in China than that of public social security expenditures, since the rate of the personal income tax and its effective tax rate are low.

7 The Urban–Rural Gap and the Changed Distribution of Income and Wealth

7.1 Introduction

With the introduction of the *hukou* system and restrictions on mobility in the 1950s, urban and rural China became separated. Policies prioritised the numerical minority living in urban areas with considerably higher and more equal income than was the case for the rural majority. The large urban to rural gap had as consequence that inequality in income and wealth in China as a whole was, and still is, larger than in each of the urban and rural parts. It also means that a rather substantial part of income inequality and wealth inequality in China as a whole can be attributed to the difference in mean income and mean wealth between urban and rural China.

Since the end of the 1980s China has changed rapidly. One of the most important changes is that larger and larger proportion of the population lives in urban areas. Actually, this development means that the number of persons living in rural areas is decreasing. Figure 2 illustrates the process by showing the rate of China's population that live in an urban area. There are three curves in the figure: first for the proportion of people who have an urban *hukou*, the second also including those who have a rural *hukou*, the migrant population. The third curve shows the natural growth rate for people with urban *hukou*. The figure illustrates that the proportion people in China living in urban areas increased continually from 27 per cent in 1988 to 65 per cent in 2021. It also shows that the migrant population has become rather huge.

This section is about how the gap in income and wealth between urban and rural China has developed since the end of the 1980s, a topic we started to

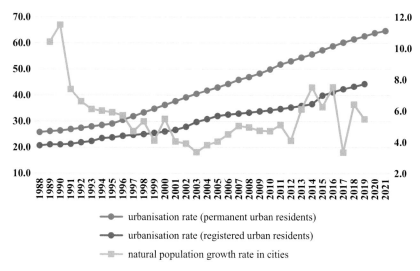

Figure 2 The urbanisation rate and the natural rate of population growth in urban areas (1988 to 2021)

Source: National Bureau of Statistics of China, China Population Statistics Yearbook, China Population and Employment Statistics Yearbook, China City Statistical Yearbook. Note: Permanent urban residents refer to residents who live in urban areas for more than six months. Registered urban residents refer to people who have urban *hukou*.

discuss in Section 5. It also deals with the importance of those gaps for inequality in income and wealth in China as a whole and for how those inequalities have developed. We also deal with changes in some other circumstances important for the distribution of income and wealth in China.

7.2 The Urban–Rural Income and Wealth Gaps

Since the end of the 1980s the restrictions on rural people to enter the cities have lessened. As consequence of this and in combination with the large urban–rural income gap, the number of people with rural *hukou* living in urban areas increased rapidly to become very large.

The rural to urban migrants typically worked many hours and saved a large proportion of their income. Much of the rural to urban migration is, and still is, temporary as many workers return to their rural origin after a period in a city. Such migration can foster rural development if the migrant has acquired productive knowledge in a city and/or has accumulated savings that are used for productive purposes. Rural to urban migration that has taken place during one period can therefore lead to higher rural income during later periods. Furthermore, while for many years migrant workers typically earned low hourly wages, this has recently changed. The qualifications of migrant workers have increased as the education level of young rural workers improved. Migrants' wages are likely to increase more rapidly than those of urban residents when the supply of migrant workers is no longer 'unlimited'; see the discussion in Section 5.

During the period we study here, there have also been changes in public policy. The 'National New-Type Urbanisation Plan (2014 to 2020)' ('Guo Jia Xin Xing Cheng Zhen Hua Gui Hua') of the central government aimed to reduce the number of rural *hukou* holders living in urban areas by converting their *hukou*. It also aimed to increase rural migrants' entitlement in terms of health care, training, and education of their children. The central government issued directives to smaller and medium cities to abolish the *hukou* system entirely. However, those directives on *hukou* reform have been followed only to varying degrees. Also, some rural residents have for various reasons been hesitant to convert their *hukou* status. Such changes have affected small- and medium-sized cities rather than the large cities. As the largest cities offer the most and best employment opportunities, they are usually the most attractive for potential migrants.

The urban to rural wealth ratio has changed over time, changes that are different from the income ratio. Many urban households could benefit from housing reform as they were given rights to buy housing from work units at low prices and thereby made capital gains. Furthermore, Chinas' rapid urbanisation has led to increased demand for housing in urban areas. As a consequence, market prices of urban housing, on average the most important component of private wealth in urban China, have increased very rapidly. Furthermore, the average urban household receives a much higher income than the average rural household and can therefore save more, which has as consequence increased household wealth during later periods, see Knight, Li and Wan (2022).

7.3 How Have the Urban–Rural Income and Wealth Ratios Changed? What the Data Show

Several measurement issues must first be addressed. What is classified as 'urban' and 'rural' is not entirely fixed as predominantly due to in-migration some rural areas have been reclassified as 'urban'. Figure 3 shows selected estimates of how the urban–rural income ratio has evolved from 1988 to 2021. We can say how the urban to rural income gap has developed during the three decades according to official statistics. First it tended to increase, to reach a maximum during the years 2007 and 2009 when the average urban–rural income ratio was as high as 3.3. Thereafter, the urban–rural income ratio has tended to decrease. In 2021, the officially reported ratio had changed to 2.5, although one part of the reduction (0.2 units) is due to changes in definitions. However, according to the same figure, in 2021 the urban to rural gap remained slightly larger than in 1988.

The data from CHIP have a more comprehensive definition of income than do the official (NBS) data. Changes in the urban to rural income ratio have been larger for CHIP than for NBS; see Figure 3. The CHIP surveys also make it possible to compare the level of average income among the three categories: rural to urban migrants, urban residents, and rural residents. Such comparisons show that on average rural to urban migrant households received much higher income than rural resident households. This indicates that rural to urban migration has on average benefitted from the move. However, the average income of rural to urban migrants was for most of the period considerably lower than the average income of urban residents. A recent development is that this seems no longer to be the case in 2018.

The data from CHIP also makes it possible to inspect the size and development of the urban to rural wealth gap, which is not reported by NBS. Figure 3

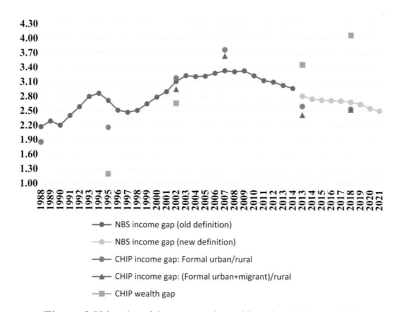

Figure 3 Urban/rural income and wealth ratio (1988 to 2021)

Source: NBS income measurement is from NBS yearbooks (www.stats.gov.cn/english/ Statisticaldata/AnnualData/).

NBS (old income definition) is from the 1999–2014 NBS yearbooks.

NBS (new income definition) is from NBS yearbooks from 2015 onward. CHIP income measurement is based on CHIP survey data 1988, 1995, 2002, 2007, 2013, and 2018. Estimate of CHIP wealth gap in 1995 is from Li and Zhao (2007). Estimates of CHIP wealth gap in 2002, 2013, and 2018 are from Wan and Knight (2023).

shows a clear upward trend. It started from a level lower than the urban to rural income gap to become larger than it.

7.4 Income Inequality and Household Wealth at the Household Level: How Has It Changed?

We now turn to the development of inequality in income and inequality in wealth according to CHIP. The Gini coefficient is probably the most frequently used measure of income inequality and wealth inequality. Figure 4 shows how the Gini coefficients for China as a whole developed from 1988 to 2018.

Seen from an international perspective, the distribution of household wealth in China was remarkably equal in 1988. Indeed, there was very little private wealth. Thereafter, wealth inequality has increased greatly. According to CHIP data the increase from 2002 to 2013 was large, but thereafter wealth inequality increased only slightly. The Gini coefficient was 0.50 in 2002, 0.61, eleven years later, in 2013, and 0.63, five years later, in 2018. The development of income inequality, as measured by the Gini coefficient, is similar, but less dramatic. Actually, according to other inequality indices computed from the same microdata, there was a slight decrease in income inequality from 2013 to 2018. The recent development of income inequality in China has received attention among researchers; see Piketty et al. (2019) and Kanbur et al. (2021), and for a survey, see Zhang (2021).

When disaggregating China into urban and rural parts one finds that income is more unequally distributed in the rural parts of the country than in the urban parts. Relatively much of rural income inequality is due to households living in eastern China, having higher mean income than those living in central or western China.

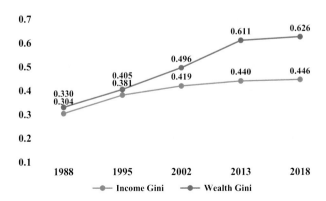

Figure 4 National income and wealth Gini coefficient
Source: Wan, Gustafsson, and Wang (2022).

Table 6 Income inequality decomposition by urban and rural subgroups using mean logarithmic deviation

	1988	1995	2002	2013	2018
Total	0.194	0.319	0.365	0.328	0.328
Between	0.040	0.067	0.143	0.091	0.096
Within	0.154	0.252	0.222	0.237	0.232
Total	100	100	100	100	100
Between	**20.5**	**20.9**	**39.1**	**27.8**	**29.3**
Within	79.5	79.1	60.9	72.2	70.8

Notes: Calculated using CHIP income definition. Rural to urban migrants are included in urban sample.

An important part of Chinese income inequality is the difference in income levels between urban and rural areas. Because the Gini coefficient is not additively decomposable, we use the mean logarithmic deviation (MLD). Using this index, total inequality in China is equal to the sum of population weighted inequality in rural areas and the population weighted inequality in urban areas plus a term showing the importance of the gap in income between the urban and rural areas.

Several comments can be made on Table 6 and its relationship to what is reported in Figure 4. First, definitions and the choice of inequality measure can matter. According to Table 6 the increase in income inequality came to a halt in 2002, not in 2013, as it did according to the Gini coefficient and assumptions used to make Figure 4. A second and more substantial comment is that the difference in mean income between urban and rural China has large but varying importance for income inequality in China as a whole. In 1988, 20.5 per cent of income inequality measured by MLD could be attributed to differences in mean income, weighted by population shares, between urban and rural China. This proportion had increased to as much as 39.1 per cent in 2002. However, in 2013 the corresponding proportion was down to 27.8 per cent of income inequality in China as a whole. There are most probably many reasons for the changes. One of those is changes in the volume and composition of rural to urban migrants.

That average income in urban China is substantially higher than in rural China can to a large extent be attributed to the policies that were introduced in China as early as in the 1950s, which prioritised the urban regions at the expense of rural regions. The analysis of Sicular et al. (2007) finds that education had played an important role. If rural people had acquired the same length of education as urban people, the urban to rural income ratio would have been reduced by approximately one-fourth.

7.5 Conclusions

From 1988 to about 2013 China's income inequality at the household level increased. Wealth inequality has continued to do so after 2013, although the pace has slowed. It is also true that despite large increases the distribution of wealth in China is not as unequal as its counterpart in many rich countries. The reason is that almost all Chinese rural *hukou* holders 'own' both some land and a house, and in addition house ownership is widespread among urban *hukou* holders.

The urban to rural income ratio is large in China. Its change over thirty years has had huge consequences for the change in China's income inequality. There was a tendency for the ratio to decrease in recent years, causing income inequality in China as a whole to flatten out. Furthermore, public policy has recently changed in a way which meant that the type of *hukou* a person has lost importance in small- and medium-sized cities. As more and more people live in China's urban areas, the urban–rural income ratio becomes less important in determining the degree of income inequality in China as a whole.

8 The Development of Inequality of Opportunities and Poverty

8.1 Introduction

In this section, we continue to look at the development of household income in China, but now from two other angles. One is the relatively new perspective of IOp. Much of the work on this topic is inspired by Roemer's (1998) observation that some inequality is due to factors under the control of the individual because of his or her efforts and choices. This reflects inequality for which the individual can be held responsible. However, some inequality is due to factors that are beyond the individual's control, that is circumstances and opportunities. This part reflects inequality for which the individuals should not be held responsible. This raises an empirical question: has IOp in China increased or decreased? We will address this question for the period 2002–2018 in Sections 8.2 and 8.3.

In the other parts of this section we will focus on people with lesser means: China's income-poor. As we will discuss in Section 8.4, there are official assessments of how many people are poor in China's rural areas and also assessments of the public policies intended to eradicate this poverty. In Section 8.5, using official criteria, we report on how rural poverty has declined and on how it is affected by public transfers. By contrast, when households in urban China are approaching a standard of living prevailing in high-income countries, criteria for defining poverty similar to those used in such countries will become relevant. What consequences this will have for mapping the extent and profile of poverty among urban people will be discussed in Section 8.6.

8.2 Why Study IOp?

For long, sociologists have studied how social position as measured by class or prestige is related across generations. The equivalent in economics is to analyse intergenerational relations in income and education. There are now some studies of intergenerational income mobility in China. For example, Deng et al. (2013), using CHIP data for 1995 and 2002, find that the strength of the son–father relation in urban China is stronger than that reported for several high-income countries with large welfare states. The strength of this income link in urban China appears to be not very different from what has been reported for Brazil, Chile, and the United States.

Inequality of opportunities is a broader concept than intergenerational mobility as it allows childhood's long-run consequences to be characterised by more than one variable. Furthermore, it is flexible with respect to the measure of inequality.

There are several studies aiming to quantify IOp for different countries, and different methods have been used. Yang et al. (2021) have investigated China and have added one new study, which investigates changes in IOp for persons aged twenty-six to fifty from 2002 to 2018, a period longer and more recent than in previous studies of China. The three waves of CHIP data that are used contain rich information. Yang et al. (2021) analyse also how IOp within birth cohorts changes with age, and how IOp differs across birth cohorts.

8.3 How Has IOp in China Developed?

A main finding of the authors is that the level of IOp and its contribution to total inequality in China declined from 2013 to 2018 (Table 7). In 2018, the level of IOp in China was in the middle-to-low range of countries. It was lower than for most middle- and lower-income countries, somewhat higher than in the United Kingdom and United States, and considerably higher than in the Nordic countries.

Table 7 Nationwide total inequality and inequality of opportunity. Estimates based on the Gini coefficient

Row / Year		2002	2013	2018
A	Total inequality	0.392	0.426	0.440
B	Inequality of opportunities	0.156	0.156	0.113
C	Ratio of inequality of opportunity to total inequality (B/A), per cent	39.9	36.7	25.7

Source: Yang et al. (2021). The results relate to persons aged twenty-six to fifty.

The results also suggest that much of the recent decline in IOp in China is associated with reductions in the IOp of specific circumstance variables. The decline also reflects the fact that IOp has fallen across generations. IOp associated with region of residence and *hukou* at birth declined. This underlines the importance of ongoing reductions in barriers to mobility, for example, through reforms of the *hukou* system and also the recent reduction of the gap in income between urban and rural areas. However, IOp associated with parents' education increased. The latter is consistent with the relationship between a persons' length of education and her or his earnings becoming stronger than during the planning epoque.

8.4 How Poverty Is Defined and Combated in Rural China

There have been three official poverty standards in China, set in 1978, 2008, and 2010. They all relate to rural China, not to households and individual living in urban China. The National Bureau of Statistics updates the rural poverty standard annually according to the rural residents' consumer price index. The updated poverty line is used to measure the poverty headcount ratio of the year. In this section, the poverty standard of 2,300 yuan in 2010 is used to measure the poverty indexes. Taking the consumer price index and other factors into account, we converted the (annual per person) poverty line in 2002, 2013, and 2018 to 1,797 yuan, 2,736 yuan, and 2,995 yuan, respectively.

Table 8 reports the rural poverty headcount ratios in China in 2002, 2013, and 2018 based on both income poverty measures and consumption poverty measures. It shows that the poverty headcount ratio in rural China significantly decreased from 2002 to 2018, measured either by income or by consumption, indicating poverty reduction over these years.[9]

Table 8 Rural poverty headcount ratios, 2002–18 (per cent)

Welfare measure	2002	2013	2018
Income	35.75	8.90	3.43
Consumption	64.70	7.96	1.28

Source: Chong, Cai, and Yue (2022).

---

[9] Consistent with this development a decreasing number of rural people are living in households with consumption or income below the global poverty line used by the World Bank or the official poverty line of the Chinese government, see for example Chen and Ravallion (2021).

The prime reason for this development is the rapid increase in income for residents of rural China over the decades. Public policy has contributed to this, through several specific measures. They include measures to direct resources to areas defined as poor. Such areas were first defined at the county level but since 2001 at the village level. However, an evaluation of poverty alleviation measures directed at the village during the first years showed mixed results (Park and Wang, 2010). For example, it should be understood that there is substantial income inequality among households within poor villages.

More recently, the Chinese central government has implemented the Targeted Poverty Alleviation (TPA) policy nationwide. This includes activities for each beneficiary household by developing personalised measures to improve their standard of living and development ability. The specific objective of the TPA was by 2020 to lift all rural people (82.5 million in 2013) over the absolute poverty line as it was defined in 2010. Various public organisations have been given responsibilities for this poverty alleviation work in the designed areas, and the funds used have been rather large.[10]

8.5 The Poverty Reduction Effect of Some Public Policies in Rural China in 2002, 2013, and 2018

The question we intend to answer in this section is: to what extent have various government transfer policies reduced rural poverty headcount ratios? We do this by comparing measures of poverty as calculated before and after considering the value of government transfers. We measure the poverty reduction effects of five single public transfer policies (pensions, *dibao*, a social assistance programme, medical expense reimbursements, cash benefits for farmers, and other public transfers) and the cumulative effects of those transfer policies.[11]

Table 9 reports the poverty reduction effects of different types of public transfer income from 2002 to 2018, whose effect in 2018 was the most significant. In 2018, the poverty headcount ratio before the public transfer was 7.99 per cent; it decreased to 3.43 per cent after considering the different government transfers. Thus, according to this calculation, the poverty headcount ratio was reduced by 4.56 per cent due to public social security programmes. This can be compared with that in 2002, government transfers reduced the poverty headcount ratio by only 0.97 per cent. Thus, the poverty-reducing effect of public transfers, having

---

[10] See for example Bikales (2021).

[11] The single policy effect is measured by adding each public transfer to the pre-transfer income, respectively. The cumulative effect of transfer policies is measured by adding the different kinds of government transfers successively to the pre-transfer income until the sum is equal to the disposable income.

Table 9 Poverty reduction effects of different types of transfer income, rural China (per cent)

Types of income	2002	Decrease rate	2013	Decrease rate	2018	Decrease rate
Pre-transfer income	36.72	–	12.90	–	7.99	–
Pre-transfer income + pension	36.54	0.18	10.85	2.05	5.26	2.73
Pre-transfer income + *dibao*	36.72	–	12.43	0.47	7.36	0.63
Pre-transfer income + medical expense reimbursement	–	–	12.52	0.38	7.31	0.68
Pre-transfer income + cash benefits for farmers	36.15	0.57	12.02	0.88	7.17	0.82
Pre-transfer income + other public transfers	36.52	0.20	12.28	0.62	7.03	0.96
Pre-transfer income + public transfers	35.75	0.97	8.90	4.00	3.43	4.56

Source: Chong, Cai, and Yue (2022).

Note: Pensions include the formal sector pension (including the urban employee pension), the urban resident pension, and the new rural social pension. Disposable income equals the sum of pre-transfer income, pension, *dibao*, medical expense reimbursement, cash benefits for farmers, and other public transfer incomes.

been negligible at the start of the period studied here, was considerably strengthened during the period.

Different government transfers have different effects on poverty. In 2002, the poverty reduction effect of cash benefits for farmers was the largest, 0.57 per cent. At that time, pensions took no more than 0.18 per cent of the rural population out of poverty but, in 2018, 2.73 per cent. The reason for the change is that the government has increased the coverage as well as the benefits of rural pensions.

8.6 Poverty in Urban China

'Poverty' can be conceptualised in different ways. As stated above there is no official poverty line for urban China. However, several authors have made efforts to map the extent and profile of urban poverty in China, see for example Meng et al. (2005) and Appleton et al. (2010). There are efforts to consider not only income and consumption when deeming whether a person is to be considered poor. A recent effort to use the multidimensional approach when studying child poverty in China is Shen and Alkire (2022).

As the general income level in urban China has been rising rapidly, why not define poverty as an income level relative to the general income level prevailing in this particular society? When income increases over a subsistence level, people become concerned about their income relative to the income of others in the same society. For example, this is the case when assessing income poverty in the European Union: the cut-off defining who are (relatively) poor is most often set at income less than 60 per cent of the median per capita income level in the studied population.

Gustafsson and Ding (2020) applied this 60 per cent of median measure of the urban households' poverty line to the income of urban residents as measured in CHIP data for the years 1988–2013. They found that the proportion of urban residents living in households with less than 60 per cent of the contemporary median income tripled during this period. In 2013, it stood at 20 per cent – a rate somewhat higher than the rate reported for the EU as a whole. Those authors also reported that relative poverty rates for urban residents in China were similar to those reported for Hong Kong. However, these rates are higher than in several rich countries. Consequently, it matters a great deal through which lens poverty in urban China is observed. If assessed by standards that have been applied to rural China, there is nowadays very little poverty in urban China. However, by the criterion employed in many high-income countries, relative poverty is a substantial and increasing problem in urban China. Note also that today most people in China live in an urban area.

Gustafsson and Ding (2020) also demonstrated that if one or more adult household members are not employed at all or during parts of the year, then this increases the risk of relative poverty. Circumstances in the household that lead to an increased risk of being poor were found to be that a household head had a low level of educational attainment, and that the household was living in a low-income city. Other circumstances that lead to an increased risk of being relatively poor were a large number of children, as well as the number of elderly people without a pension. From this, it follows that policies that increase employment rates of adults and the level of educational attainment have the potential to reduce relative poverty in urban China.

8.7 Conclusions

We have looked at different ways to evaluate how the population in China has fared since the end of the 1980s. Approaching the issue from the perspective of IOp, China has made substantial progress between the years 2013 and 2018. This is primarily caused by the fact that the importance of where a person was born and grew up has diminished. However, working in the other direction, the importance of parents' education has increased.

Judged by the official poverty line, or the world poverty line as used by the World Bank, rapidly rising rural incomes have dramatically reduced rural poverty in China. This reduction, between 1988 and 2018, was actually more rapid than in any other large- or medium-sized population in the world. China's rapid income growth is the major explanation why global poverty, as assessed by the World Bank, has decreased.

However, rapidly rising urban incomes raise the question: should urban poverty now be measured using the approach accepted in high-income countries? We have shown that although they have higher incomes than before, an increasing number of households in the bottom of the urban income distribution have fallen behind and become relatively poor.

9 Inequality by Gender and Ethnicity

9.1 Introduction

When the CPC came to power the new government brought ambitious ideas influencing policies regarding social rights for women, particularly for those living in urban areas. The new government also had higher ambitions regarding the situation of ethnic minorities. In this section, we look closely at how inequality along those two dimensions – gender and ethnicity – has developed since the end of the 1980s.

9.2 Understanding the Development of the Aggregate Gender Wage Gap

In the cities, where a minority of China's population has lived during a long period in history, almost all men and women became employed in SOEs or in collectives. The policy during the 1950s was very much inspired by arrangements in the Soviet Union, at that time a model for Chinese policymakers. Wage inequality was by most standards extremely small. A comparison of wage inequality in the Soviet Union and China at the end of the 1980s, when the planned economy dominated in both countries, showed that it was similar in urban China and urban Russia. On the one hand, the gender wage gap, to the disadvantage of female workers, was considerably smaller in urban China than in Russia. On the other hand, age – indicating seniority – played a larger role in wage levels in urban China (Gustafsson et al., 2001) Those results applied to people living in the cities, whereas in rural China wage employment was for long the exception (Section 3). In rural China patriarchic values were deep-seated and had huge consequences for daily life.

When China started to move towards a market economy, urban women and men were differently affected, with consequences for the urban gender wage gap. Three different approaches illustrate this – approaches that are not necessary conflicting. First is to look at the consequences of increased wage inequality only. Female workers in urban China, as in many other countries, tend to have a lower position in the wage distribution than do men. When the wage distribution became wider, a consequence was that the average female wage fell in relation to the average male wage. Alternatively expressed, the gender wage gap increased as women were 'swimming against the tide'.

A second way to look at the development of the gender wage gap in urban China concerns economic transformation. There were radical changes in the composition of ownership in the economy. Starting in the 1990s, and for many years since, the importance of the state-owned sector diminished. Political objectives to secure a small gender wage difference can be effective in the state-owned sector but are less effective in the growing private sector, where traditional gender norms play a larger role in wage determination. Thus, the changed ownership composition of employment in urban China led to an increased gender wage gap.

A third way to approach the development of the gender wage gap in urban China is to contrast services provided by households instead of the state, by focusing on the gender division of work (market work and housework). In pre-reform urban China, publically owned enterprises provided many services such as day care for young children at low or no cost. Enterprise reforms had several consequences of importance for households and their decision-making. A large number of workers became redundant. As at that time women were on average less qualified than men and the decreased urban employment had profound gender consequences. Enterprise reform also diminished the supply of services that enterprises supplied for free or at low cost to employees, and the alternative of buying market services was more expensive. It became socially more acceptable for middle-aged and older women to leave the labour force, for instance to provide care for grandchildren or older persons. In addition, it was public policy to introduce measures like early retirement in order to compensate middle-aged and older workers who became redundant. A majority of those benefits were taken up by women.

9.3 What Research and the Surveys Show

There are now a large number of published studies on how gender differences in urban, and to some extent also in rural, China has developed since the 1980s. The literature is large enough to become the object of research. Iwasaki and Ma (2020) attempt to draw conclusions by conducting a meta-analysis covering not less than 199 studies relating to the period 1978–2018. Three conclusions are drawn: first, although the gender wage gap in China is statistically significant and economically meaningful, it remains low from an international perspective. For example, although having increased, at the start of the new millennium, the gender wage gap in urban China continued to be lower than its counterpart in urban Russia (see also Gustafsson et al., 2015). Second, wage discrimination against women in China differs by location and ownership sector. It is more severe in rural than in urban China and is larger in privately owned enterprises than in SOEs. Third, the studies strongly suggest that the gender wage gap in China has increased dramatically during the transition towards a market economy and has reached the level found in high-income countries.

We will now use CHIP data to illustrate the development of gender wage differences in urban China from 1988 to 2018. Figure 5 shows that the aggregated gender wage gap increased rapidly between 1995 and 2012. In 1995, average earnings of women stood at 74 per cent of average wages of men, but in 2013 the proportion had decreased to 59 per cent.

Figure 6 shows how employment rates for women and men in urban China changed, again from 1988 to 2018. This supplements the figure showing the aggregate gender wage gap. It illustrates that employment rates among women fell rapidly from 1995 to 2013, and gap of the employment rates between men and women enlarged over years.

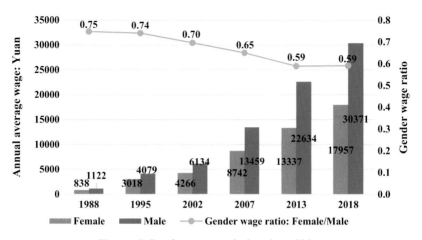

Figure 5 Gender wage ratio in urban China

Source: Calculated using CHIP survey data.

Note: The gender wage rate is computed for observations with a positive wage.

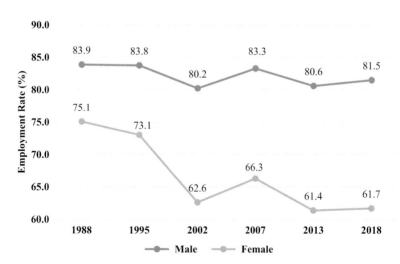

Figure 6 Employment rates for women and men in urban China

Source: Calculated using CHIP survey data.

Note: Employment rates are calculated as the ratio of the employed to the working age population. Employed people are those aged sixteen to sixty, who report that they have worked in gainful employment during the reference year. The working age population refers to people aged sixteen to sixty.

9.4 The Meaning of Ethnicity in China

In one sense ethnicity is an unambiguous concept in present-day China. On the identification card that all people in China possess, one out of fifty-six alternatives is stated. Most people are classified as Han, a category making up 91.1 per cent of China's population, numbering 1,410 million persons in 2020. The remaining 8.9 per cent, or 125 million persons, are ethnic minorities (NBS, 2021). The ethnic minorities are more concentrated in rural areas than the ethnic majority.

The ethnic classification of the population can be traced to the 1950s after the CPC had come to power. The classification was influenced by similar arrangements in the Soviet Union and also based on fieldwork in which minorities' social history, economic life, language, and religion were investigated (see Mullaney, 2011). During the classification process a number of considerations were taken into account. The process could lead to people who spoke different languages being brought together into one category. This applies not only to some minority categories but also to the Han category.

Table 10 lists the twelve most numerous ethnic minorities by their name and number of members, and it also indicates their spatial concentration. China's largest ethnic minority is the Zhuang, who mostly live in the south of China. Almost all Uighur and Hui are Muslims. The former, visibly different from the

Table 10 The population size of the largest ethnic minorities in China 2020 and their spatial concentration

Name	Number of persons, millions	Spatial concentration
Zhuang	19.6	South
Uighur	11.8	North-West
Hui	11.4	North
Miao	11.1	South-West
Manchu	10.4	North-East
Yi	9.8	South-West
Tujia	9.6	South-West
Tibetan	7.1	West
Mongol	6.3	North
Dong	3.5	South-West
Yao	3.3	South-West
Bai	2.1	South-West

Source: Seventh National Population Census 2020 as reported in Statistical Yearbook of China 2021.

Han, are concentrated to Xinjiang, which during the Republic of China era was not firmly under the control of the central government. Similar in the latter respect, and also visibly different from the majority, are the Tibetans who are concentrated to Tibet. The south-west of China is the home of many ethnic minorities. The largest are the Miao, Yi, Tujia, Dong, Yao, and Bai. In the north-east one finds most of the Manchurians, who during centuries of Imperial rule were the rulers of China. Also the Mongols, who live concentrated in the north, played a large role in China's history. This description indicates that China's ethnic minorities are a heterogeneous category.

A number of policies in present-day China are focused on the ethnic minorities. A major instrument is the administrative autonomy of areas where many minority people live. Those areas have limited administrative autonomy but can design their own laws and regulations. Within this framework resources from the budget of the central government can be, and have been, directed to areas where many ethnic minority people live. Minority ethnic policies include, for example, measures to promote education.

9.5 What Research Shows

There has been little research aiming to map and understand ethnic disparities in income and poverty in contemporary China. One reason is the lack of rich microdata covering both ethnic minorities and the Han majority. Here we first concentrate on results based on data from the CHIP. An early such study is Gustafsson and Li, (2003), who analysed the income disparity between rural persons living in minority households as an aggregate and the Han majority for the years 1988 and 1995. The authors reported a widening ethnic income disparity between the two years. This development could be attributed to the more rapid income growth in the eastern part of China, which in turn could be linked to China's policy of first opening up the eastern region. Interestingly, this mechanism might later have worked in reverse. This is illustrated by results reported by Gustafsson and Zhang (2023). Those authors studied, among other things, how the rural income gap between the Yi minority and the Han majority declined from 2002 to 2018.

The CHIP data for 2002 allowed studying ethnic minorities belonging to some specific minorities and the Han. We will discuss two out of several examples. One is Gustafsson and Ding (2009a), who aggregated information at the village level and reported a substantial variation in mean income and mean wealth across the investigated ethnic groups. The average for Manchurian villages was in a slightly better position than the average for Han villages, which in turn had a considerably higher average income than villages inhabited by each of the Miao, Yi, and Zhuang ethnic minorities. Several reasons for those differences were found, but location was the single most important.

Another example of using this data is Gustafsson and Ding (2009b), who investigated rural poverty in a dynamic setting. This study showed that using the National Bureau of Statistics' low-income line, almost one-third of the ethnic minorities experienced poverty at least once during a three-year period, while the corresponding proportion among the Han majority was only approximately half as high. Nevertheless, by far most of the poor in rural China belong to the, numerically much larger, ethnic majority.

There are some studies of the urban labour market in China and ethnicity. For example, members of several ethnic minorities (Mongolian and particular Uighur and Tibetan) are less attractive to hire than Han applicants (Maurer-Fazio, 2012). Some studies have analysed the 2005 China Inter-Census Survey to examine ethnic differences in the urban labour market. One example is Gustafsson and Yang (2017), who studied nine different minority ethnicities. On average, male urban ethnic minority workers earned 11 per cent less than Han workers, while for female workers the gap was no more than 5 per cent. Those numbers are much lower than many ethnic income gaps reported for rural China. Looking at particular minorities the authors found examples of three different changes over time in earnings premiums and earnings penalties for urban workers: one ethnic minority for whom the development has been more favourable than for the Han majority; a second category in which development has been similar; and a third category for which development has been unfavourable. Thus, it can be misleading to infer the experience of one ethnic minority from that of another.

There are also studies that have used the China Household Ethnic Survey, which collected data for ethnic minorities and Han households in seven regions in western China in 2011 (see Gustafsson et al., 2021). The main findings in this volume were that ethnic-related gaps in household income differ from rather marginal to substantial in the rural parts of the seven regions. They are in most, but not all, cases to the disadvantage of ethnic minorities. There is considerable heterogeneity regarding behaviour and economic situation across China's ethnic minorities. Poverty is a large problem for several of China's rural ethnic minorities. Mandarin-related skills and economic situation are positively related. Recent pro-rural policies have had mixed consequences for ethnic inequalities. Ethnic minorities tend to be less likely than the Han people to migrate from rural to those urban areas in which ethnic disparities in the labour market exist.

9.6 Conclusions

The evidence is clear that the gender wage gap in urban China has increased from an internationally seen low level since the start of economic reform in the 1990s. The development of increased gender wage gap is contrary to what most developed countries have experienced during the same period. The fact that the gender wage gap has increased in urban China can be given several, not necessarily mutually exclusive, explanations: earning inequality has increased, the composition of ownership sectors has changed, and there has been interplay between economic transformation and gender division of paid and unpaid work.

Members of several, but not all, ethnic minorities in rural China have a less favourable economic situation than average members of the Han majority. Much, but not all, of these differences can be attributed to the fact that many ethnic minority persons live in places that are less developed than where most Han people live. However, there is also evidence of workers of some ethnic minorities being unfavourably treated when searching for jobs.

10 The Growth of China's Middle Class

10.1 Introduction

In 2022, China's GDP is the second largest in the world after the United States. In purchasing power parity (PPP) terms, China's GDP is already the largest in the world. The rapid economic growth has led to very rapid improvements in the living standards of China's population. As a consequence, an increasing number of China's people have lives that resemble those of a majority in the developed countries. They can, for example, afford eating meals out regularly, travel for a holiday, and own an automobile.

A well-off consumer class has emerged in China. The earlier focus in the official rhetoric on peasants and workers has been replaced by an emphasis on those having high cultural capital and the economic capacity to consume (Goodman, 2014). The expansion of a middle class can also have consequences reaching beyond private consumption. Examples include improved governance, better delivery of public services, and the empowerment of civil society. An increased size of the middle class could also affect how political decisions are made. Furthermore, owing to its large population, China's middle-class population could, measured in size, overtake the middle-class populations of Western countries. Therefore, it will be able to influence the kinds of goods and services that are demanded worldwide. There are thus several reasons to ask: how has the size of the Chinese middle class grown, what are its characteristics, and how does it compare to the size of the middle class in other countries?

10.2 The Meaning and Measurement of China's Global Middle Class

'Middle class' is a word often used, but it can be given different meanings. Academic approaches vary and depend on the discipline and theoretical perspective of the authors, see for example Gustafsson et al. (2020). Sociological studies usually view class as being related to one's position in the production process, social group identification, and/or attitudes. Empirical studies based on these concepts typically employ multiple variables. Economic studies define the middle class in terms of one's command over resources or ability to consume. The variable used to identify membership in the middle class is usually household income or consumption expenditures. Classification of individuals as middle class is relatively straightforward in that it depends on one single variable. Researchers must decide, however, where to set the cut-off between the middle class and other classes.

The definition used here is based on the income of a person's household. It is suitable for comparisons over time and across countries and is influenced by previous research that has not focused on China: see for example Milanovic and Yitzhaki (2002) and Kharas (2017). If the person lived in a high-income country and household income regarded him or her as neither poor nor affluent, she or he was here labelled 'middle class'. More precisely, a person living in the European Union in a household with a disposable income in the interval 60–200 per cent of the median for the EU is classified 'middle class', Gustafsson et al. (2020). The 60 per cent of the median criterion is used as a poverty line in many official documents from the European Union.

The information on the two cut-offs were derived from the Luxembourg Income Study (LIS). In that research project microdata from more than fifty high- and middle-income countries are assembled and harmonised. In this section, we use this database to report the size of the middle class in selected countries other than China. For China we use the CHIP surveys.

Although conceptually clear, several operational assumptions have to be made before arriving at what is reported in this section. One is that we convert amounts of income that are reported in local currency in the LIS data sets to a common currency and also common year's prices. Another key assumption is that we anchor the middle-class criterion on incomes in the EU that were observed in 2018.

10.3 How China's Global Middle Class Has Risen and What Characterises It

The assumptions made and data estimates of China's middle class can be found in Sicular et al. (2022). In 2018, 344 million persons living in China were considered middle class. They comprise 25 per cent of China's population. In contrast, as few as 7.5 million belonged to the Chinese middle class in 2002, when they made up less than 1 per cent of the population. The Chinese middle class, from being a tiny minority of the population, has grown rapidly. During this sixteen-year period, annual growth of the members of the Chinese middle class averaged as much as 27 per cent. Thus, while GDP per capita grew rapidly during those years, the size of the middle class grew even more rapidly.

What characterises the Chinese middle class? With few exceptions, middle-class persons live in the urban areas of the country. This echoes the large urban to rural income gap that was discussed in earlier parts of the Element. Information in Sicular et al. (2022) shows that among individuals who in 2018 were classified as middle class, as many as 74 per cent had an urban *hukou*. In addition, 19 per cent had a rural *hukou* but lived in an urban location: they were rural to urban migrants. No more than the remaining 7 per cent of middle-class individuals lived in rural China.

Most middle-class households receive their income from wages and a substantial number from pensions, which in turn is linked to past employment. For example, in 2013 no less than 71 per cent of middle-class household's income came from such sources (Gustafsson et al., 2020). In contrast, on average no more than 13 per cent of middle-class household income came from business in 2013. It follows that China's middle class is, in general, a salaried rather than an entrepreneurial class.

Chinas' middle class is characterised by being rather large savers. In 2013, middle-class households saved as much as 34 per cent of their income. This is a much higher proportion than the saving rate of 15 per cent in the lower classes (Gustafsson et al., 2020). The saving rate of China's middle-class households is also high compared to saving rates observed for the population in rich countries.

In terms of geographical and family background, one can distinguish between different pathways to reach the middle class. Being born with an urban *hukou* provides a huge advantage. Nearly 40 per cent of this group had in 2013 attained the global middle class. Having grown up in a household with favourable characteristics, like parents with a longer education, raised the probability of being middle class still further. The main pathway to the middle class was through well-paying wage employment that provided generous pensions benefits (Gustafsson et al., 2020).

In contrast, no more than 10 per cent of those born with a rural *hukou* became middle class as adults. For them three different routes to the middle class can be identified. The odds of becoming middle class were highest if they had migrated to an urban area and also – which was difficult – had converted to urban *hukou* status. Like their urban-born middle-class neighbours, most *hukou* converters belonging to the middle class had become wage earners or pensioners. Lower odds for becoming middle class were found for those who had migrated to an urban area but kept their rural *hukou*. The lowest odds, not more than 4 per cent, were observed for people born in a rural area who also stayed rural. Many taking this route to a middle-class position lived in a household earning income as self-employed.

10.4 An International Comparison

How does the Chinese middle class compare with its counterparts in other countries? It is illustrative to compare both proportions of the total population and absolute numbers. Not surprisingly, Table 11 shows that in 2018 the Chinese middle class makes up a smaller proportion of population than the corresponding population in high-income countries. For example, whereas 25 per cent of the population in China was counted as middle class, the corresponding proportion in Europe was 69 per cent. Even larger is the difference when comparing the population proportions classified as having income over the higher cut-off for being middle class. Whereas the proportion of well to do persons was estimated to 11 per cent in Europe and as high as 35 per cent in the United States, the corresponding proportion in China was as low as 1 per cent.

Comparing the number of persons who belong to the internationally defined middle class, another picture is seen. The number of middle-class persons in China is estimated to be rather similar to the number in Europe, and considerably higher than the number in the United States. The Chinese middle class, although making up a proportion considerably smaller than in Europe and United States, is large in absolute number.

In Table 11, we also compare the proportion and size of the middle class in China with its counterparts in Brazil, Russia, India, South Africa, (countries which together with China make up the BRICS), and Mexico for 2018. According to those estimates, the middle class in China make up a smaller proportion of the population than in Russia, a country with a GDP per capita almost twice as high as in China. However, with this exception the middle class in China constitutes a larger proportion of population than in Brazil, South Africa, Mexico, and, particularly, India. Because of its large population, the estimated number of middle-class persons in China is much higher than in any of the other middle-income countries reported in Table 11. The large population of India makes it understandable that its middle-class population is similar to that in Russia.

Why does the proportion of middle-class persons vary across time? Results from analysing cross section data for thirty-three countries and China in 2018

Table 11 Estimated size of the middle class in China, the United States, Europe, and four BRICS countries, 2018

	Proportion of population belonging to each class (per cent)			Size of middle class (million)	GDP per capita (PPP US dollar)
	Lower class %	Middle class %	Upper class %		
China	74.3	24.7	1.1	344.2	15,614
United States	9.9	55.1	35.1	179.9	62,997
Europe	20.4	68.7	11.0	337.4	44,466
Brazil	81.1	16.1	2.8	33.8	14,951
Russia	42.9	54.2	2.9	78.2	28,764
India	94.0	6.0	0.1	80.5	6,655
South Africa	78.6	17.9	3.5	10.3	12,838

Source: Sicular et al. (2022)

provides some evidence. Not surprisingly, GDP per capita plays a major role. With higher GDP per capita, it follows that a larger proportion of the population is classified as middle class. However, the proportion of middle-class persons tends to diminish as the population with income too high for being classified middle class increases. An analysis of panel data for twenty-three countries and China provides a similar pattern.

China is still in the region where an increase of GDP per capita is associated with an increase of the middle class. From this we can predict that its middle class will continue to increase for several years. The statistical analysis reported in Sicular et al. (2022) shows that, although the level of GDP is important for the size of the middle class, other factors can also play a role. For example, the population share in China classified as middle class is higher than predicted from its level of GDP only, although the reasons for this are not very clear.

10.5 Conclusions

As a consequence of China's rapid growth, an increased number of people live lives similar to those lived by people in high-income countries. Applying the criterion that people live in households considered neither poor nor very well off to Chinese data, it was shown that the number of middle-class people in China was small in 2002 but had increased very rapidly to make up one-quarter of the population in 2018. This middle class is disproportionately concentrated in urban areas, and a large proportion are wage earners. People who grew up in urban China were much more likely as adults to be middle class than the rural-born, particularly if they had not migrated to an urban area.

In 2018, members of the Chinese middle class were as numerous as those of the European middle class, and larger than the middle class in North America. However, the proportion of Chinese upper class members is smaller than its counterpart in the United States and Europe. For the future we can predict that, if GDP continues to increase, the size of China's middle class will continue to grow for some time. This expansion of the Chinese middle class can have consequences for China and for the world. However, whether and how the growth of a Chinese middle class will affect China's political system is far from clear (Gustafsson et al., 2020). In case China's Communist Party is able to successfully capture the interest of the middle class, the growth of the Chinese middle class will not necessarily fundamentally challenge China's political system. However, even if growth of the middle class leaves the political system intact, a larger proportion of middle-class persons in the society could bring about changes in political priorities.

11 Summary and Final Comments

11.1 Summary

In this short Element we have covered many aspects of how Chinese households' and their members' lives have changed since the end of the 1980s. Our approach has been to focus mainly on studies using data from the China Household Income Study, in which we ourselves have been involved. In this section, we summarise the conclusions of the various sections.

Section 2 explained briefly why the Chinese economy has grown so fast over our period. Capital was accumulated very rapidly, and this involved great structural transformation, from a closed to an open economy, from state to private production, and from agriculture to industry. Each of these transfers meant higher productivity, and thus contributed to the growth rate. China's political economy required rapid growth in order to maintain social stability, which in turn required incentive structures at all levels of government towards that objective. This 'developmental state' helped to create a self-sustaining virtuous circle of economic growth.

Section 3 showed that rural China has experienced very large changes in employment during the three decades since the end of the 1980s. There has been a rapid flight from agriculture to wage employment or self-employment. The expansion of self-employment is impressive: rising from 2 per cent of rural adults in 1988 to 12 per cent in 2018. However, between the same two years the proportion wage earners increased from 15 per cent to 63 per cent (both percentages according to our definitions). Self-employment in rural China is an activity mainly for married men, not for married women. People who have become wage earners are younger and more educated that those who work as farmers. Moving from agriculture to wage employment or self-employment has led to higher income, particularly during the first years studied.

By comparison with China's rural reform, urban reform was slow and gradual, as discussed in Section 4. There were two main obstacles to progress. One was the vested interests of SOEs and their privileged urban workers. The other was the need for coordination of various interacting reforms – for instance, enterprise, housing, and financial reform – giving rise to problems of sequencing. Both obstacles were relevant to the slow pace – over thirty years – of moving from a labour system to a labour market, with a wage structure that has evolved to reflect the productivity of labour. However, China does not yet have a competitive labour market: there is segmentation in various policy-related ways.

In Section 5 we documented the remarkable transfer of labour from the rural areas to the urban areas of China over a period of thirty years. For twenty of those years, this occurred while the ratio of urban to rural income per capita consistently increased. This is consistent with the Lewis model and an important reason for the increase in the national Gini coefficient of income inequality. However, in recent years China's income inequality has remained fairly constant. This can be interpreted as China having passed the 'Lewis turning point'. However, the introduction of minimum wages and redistributive transfer policies might also have contributed to the increase in urban unskilled wages and in rural incomes that the Lewis model predicts.

During the planning epoque the tax systems and systems of social security were rather different for urban and rural residents. However, since then several changes have been made – towards universal coverage and increased benefit levels. Nevertheless, systems differences between rural and urban areas remain. In Section 6 we examined how the redistributive effect of public expenditures and revenues have changed since 1988. Social security transfers have become more equalising, especially during the 2000s, when China started to establish a comprehensive rural social safety network. The redistributive effect of the personal income tax is smaller than that of public social security expenditures, as many households do not pay income taxes.

From 1988 to about 2013 China's income inequality at the household level increased. In contrast, China's inequality of household wealth has continued to increase also after 2013, although the pace has slowed. These inequalities are the subject of Section 7. Despite large increases, the distribution of wealth in China is not as unequal as in many rich countries. However, the urban–rural income ratio is exceptionally large in China. Its change over thirty years has had huge consequences for China's income inequality. There has been a tendency for the ratio to decrease in recent years, causing the national Gini coefficient of income inequality to flatten out. Furthermore, public policy has recently changed in a way which means that a person's type of *hukou* has lost importance in small- and medium-sized cities. As more and more people live in the urban areas, the urban–rural income ratio becomes less important in determining the degree of income inequality in China as a whole.

In Section 8 we found that IOp for household income in China became smaller between 2002 and 2018. This was to a large extent caused by the fact that the importance of where a person was born and grew up diminished as geographic and social mobility grew. However, working in the other direction, the importance of parents' education increased. Over the same period, judged by the official poverty line or the world poverty line used by the World Bank, rural poverty fell rapidly. However, rapidly rising urban incomes raise the question: should urban poverty now be measured using the approach accepted in high-income countries? Although people at the bottom of the income distribution in urban China have higher incomes than before, they have fallen behind those at the middle of the distribution, and as a consequence relative poverty has increased in urban China.

It was found in Section 9 that the gender wage gap in urban China has increased since the start of economic reform in the 1990s. This development can be given several, not mutually exclusive, explanations: earnings inequality has increased, the composition of ownership sectors has changed, and there has been interplay between economic transformation and gender division of paid and unpaid work. The same section also found that members of several, but not all, ethnic minorities in rural China have a less favourable economic outcome than, on average, do members of the Han majority. Much, but not all, of these differences can be attributed to the fact that many ethnic minority people live in places that are less developed than those in which most Han people live.

Finally, in Section 10 we considered the fact that, as a consequence of China's rapid growth, an increased number of people live lives similar to those of people in high-income countries. The middle class in China was still small in number in 2002 but increased very rapidly to make up one-quarter of the population in 2018. It is disproportionately concentrated in urban areas, and a large proportion are wage earners. In 2018, members of the Chinese middle class were as numerous as those of the European middle class, and larger than the middle class in North America. However, the proportion of Chinese upper class members is smaller than its counterpart in the United States and Europe.

11.2 Final Comments

Many of the results presented in this Element either answer original questions or contribute original answers. The CHIP surveys are unique in offering comparable microeconomic data on China over a period as long as thirty years. Where there is a literature on a particular topic, our results generally strengthen knowledge based on other, often narrower, data sets. Although China alone is the subject of our research, in several places we have contrasted China's progress in economic transformation and income distribution with progress, or lack of it, in comparable countries. Often the contrasts arose from China's much more rapid economic growth. The need to explain the faster growth was therefore crucial. That was the point from which we began, in Section 2. The topics of these sections were chosen because they were researched by one or other of us. However, they are by no means the only topics that have been covered by members of the CHIP team of researchers. Others include detailed description and analysis of income levels and distribution over time, and their explanation; educational enrolment and attainment, and their effects; extensive poverty analysis and anti-poverty measures; more detailed tax and subsidy policies, and their effects; housing; unemployment; and health care. There is also a series of research papers on subjective well-being (or life satisfaction), its determinants and trends.

The CHIP, in its originality, consistency, and adaptability, has provided a wonderful source for understanding China's important socio-economic issues and their evolution over the reform years.[12] We salute its directors Zhao Renwei and Li Shi, without whose initiative, enterprise, and hard work it would not have happened in the first place and continued to this day. We hope that a new generation of team members, including Yue Ximing, Luo Chuliang, and Haiyuan Wan will continue the CHIP project, with its emphasis on scientific, research-oriented, data collection, and analysis. In this way the story of the evolution and change of China's fascinating economy and society can be extended systematically into the future.

---

[12] For more information on CHIP, see for example www.icpsr.umich.edu/web/ICPSR/series/243 or 中国收入分配研究院 China Institute For Income Distribution-CHIP dataset (ciidbnu.org).

Appendix

Table A1 Comparison of the CHIP survey samples for 1988–2018

	1988	1995	2002	2007	2013	2018
Rural sample						
Number of households	10,258	7,998	9,200	51,847	39,408	34,491
Number of persons	51,352	34,739	37,969	13,000	10,551	9,076
Number of provinces	28	19	22	16	15	15
Urban residents sample						
Number of households	9,009	6,931	6,835	29,262	20,331	28,685
Number of persons	31,827	21,694	20,632	10,000	6,866	9,120
Number of provinces	10	11	12	16	15	15
Rural to urban migrants sample						
Number of households	None	None	2,000	8,404	2,839	7,255
Number of persons	None	None	5,318	4,978	980	2,255
Number of provinces	None	None	12	9	15	15

Note: Samples of rural to urban migrants were, with the exception for those referring to 2013 and 2018, not drawn in identical ways.

Table A2 Population weights used in CHIP data for 1988–2018

	1988	1995	2002	2007	2013	2018
Rural	74.2	71.0	63.1	54.2	45.8	39.9
Urban	25.8	29.0	27.6	34.5	40.9	42.9
Migrant	NA	NA	9.4	11.3	13.3	17.3
East	37.5	37.5	39.0	39.9	41.5	41.6
Central	33.7	33.9	32.9	32.2	31.5	31.2
West	28.7	28.7	28.1	27.9	27.0	27.2

References

Appleton, S., Knight, J., Song, L., and Xia, Q. (2002). 'Labour retrenchment in China: Determinants and consequences'. *China Economic Review*, 13, 252–75.

Appleton, S., Song L., and Xia, Q. (2010). 'Growing out of poverty: Trends and patterns of urban poverty in China 1988–2002'. *World Development*, 38(5), 665–78.

Bikales, B. (2021). 'Reflections on poverty reduction in China', www.eda.admin .ch/dam/countries/countries-content/china/en/20210608-Poverty-Reduction-China_EN.pdf.

Cai, M., and Xu, J. (2022). 'Evaluating the redistributive effect of social security programs in China over the past 30 years'. *China & World Economy*, 30(1), 58–81.

Cai, M., and Yue, X. (2016). 'Woguo jumin shouru bupingdeng de zhuyao yuanyin: Shichang haishi zhengfu zhengce' (The main reasons for income inequality in China: Market or government policy). *Caijing yanjiu (Journal of Finance and Economics)*, 42(4), 4–14.

Chen, S., and Ravallion, M. (2021). 'Reconciling the conflicting narratives on poverty in China'. *Journal of Development Economics*, 153, 102711.

China & World Economy. (2022). *No 1 Special Issue: Development, Inequality and Common Prosperity*, edited by Shi Li and Ximing Yue. Institute of World Economics and Politics, Chinese Academy of Social Sciences (CASS) and Wiley.

Chong, C., Cai, M., and Yue, X. (2022). 'Focus shift needed: From development-oriented to social security-based poverty alleviation in rural China'. *Economic and Political Studies*, 10(1), 62–84.

Deng, Q. (2017). 'Estimating the effect of minimum wage on firm profitability in China'. *Economic and Political Studies*, 5(3), 326–41.

Deng, Q., Gustafsson, B., and Li, S. (2013). 'Intergenerational income persistency in urban China'. *Review of Income and Wealth*, 59(3), 416–36.

Dorfman, M. C., Holzmann, R., O'Keefe, P. et al. (2013). *China's Pension System: A Vision*. Washington DC: The World Bank.

Fang, T., and Lin, C. (2020). 'Minimum wages and employment in China'. In S. Li, and C. Lin (eds.), *Minimum Wages in China*, 71–112, Singapore: Palgrave Macmillan.

Feng, J., Yu, Y., and Lou P. (2015). 'Medical demand and growing medical costs in China-based on the gap between senior citizens' medical costs in urban and rural areas'. *Social Science China*, 3, 85–103.

Gao, Q., Yang, S., Zhai, F., and Wang, Y. (2019). 'Social policy reforms and economic distances in China'. In T. Sicular, S. Li, X. Yue, and H. Sato (eds.), *Changing Trends in Chinese Inequality: Evidence, Analysis, and Prospects*, 145–68, New York: Oxford University Press.

Gollin, D. (2014). 'The Lewis model: A 60-year retrospective'. *Journal of Economic Perspectives*, 28(3), 71–88.

Goodman, D. S. G. (2014). *Class in Contemporary China*, Cambridge: Polity Press.

Griffin, K., and Zhao R. (eds.) (1993). *The Distribution of Income in China*, London: Macmillan.

Gustafsson, B., and Ding, S. (2009a). 'Villages where China's ethnic minorities live'. *China Economic Review*, 20, 193–207.

Gustafsson, B., and Ding, S. (2009b). 'Temporary and persistent poverty among ethnic minorities and the majority in rural China'. *Review of Income and Wealth*, 55, 588–606.

Gustafsson, B., and Ding, S. (2020). 'Growing into relative income poverty: Urban China 1988 to 2013'. *Social Indicators Research*, 147(1), 73–94.

Gustafsson, B., Hasmath, R., and Ding, S. (eds.) (2021). *Ethnicity and Inequality in China*, Oxon: Routledge.

Gustafsson, B., and Li. S, (2003). 'The ethnic minority-majority income gap in rural China during transition'. *Economic Development and Cultural Change*, 51, 805–22.

Gustafsson, B., Li, S., and Nivorozhkina, L. (2015). 'Yuan and Roubles: Comparing wage determination in urban China and Russia at the beginning of the new millennium'. *China Economic Review*, 35, 248–65.

Gustafsson, B., Li, S., Nivorozhkina, L., and Katz, K. (2001). 'Rubles and Yuan: Wage functions for Russia and China'. *Economic Development and Cultural Change*, 50(1), 1–18.

Gustafsson, B., Li, S., and Sicular, T. (eds.) (2008). *Inequality and Public Policy in China*, New York: Cambridge University Press.

Gustafsson, B., and Wan H. (2020). 'Wage growth and inequality in urban China: 1988-2013'. *China Economic Review*, 62, 101462.

Gustafsson, B., and Yang, X. (2017). 'Earnings among nine ethnic minorities and the Han majority in China's cities'. *Journal of Asia Pacific Economy*, 22(3), 525–46.

Gustafsson, B., Yang, X., and Sicular, T. (2020). 'Catching up with the West: Chinese pathways to the global middle class'. *The China Journal*, 84, 102–27.

Gustafsson, B., and Zhang, Y. (2022). 'Self-employment in rural China: Its development, characteristics, and relation to Income'. *China & World Economy*, 30(1), 136–65.

Gustafsson, B., and Zhang, Y. (2023). 'Incomplete catching up: Income among Manchurian, Yi and Han people in rural China from 2002 to 2018'. *China Quarterly*, 253, 197–213.

Hoken, H., and Sato, H. (2019). 'Public policy and long term trends in inequality in rural China'. In T. Sicular, S. Li, X. Yue, and H. Sato (eds.), *Changing Trends in Chinese Inequality: Evidence, Analysis, and Prospects*, 169–200, New York: Oxford University Press.

Iwasaki, I., and Ma, X. (2020). 'Gender wage gap in China: A large meta-analysis'. *Journal for Labour Market Research*, 54(17). https://doi.org/10.1186/s12651-020-00279-5.

Kakwani, N. C. (1977). 'Measurement of tax progressivity: An international comparison'. *Economic Journal*, 87(345), 71–80.

Kakwani, N. C. (1984). 'On the measurement of tax progressivity and redistributive effect of taxes with applications to horizontal and vertical equity'. *Advances in Econometrics: A Research Annual*, 3, 149–68.

Kanbur, R., Wang, Y., and Zhang, X. (2021). 'The great Chinese inequality turnaround'. *Journal of Comparative Economics*, 49(2), 467–82.

Kharas, H. (2017). 'The unprecedented expansion of the global middle class: An update'. Global Economy and Development Working Paper 100, Washington: Brookings Institution.

Knight, J. (2014). 'China as a developmental state'. *The World Economy*, 37(10), 1335–47.

Knight, J. (2016). 'The societal cost of China's rapid economic growth'. *Asian Economic Papers*, 15(2), 138–59.

Knight, J. (2021). 'A tale of two countries and two stages: South Africa, China, and the Lewis model'. *South African Journal of Economics*, 89(2), 143–72.

Knight, J., Deng, Q., and Li, S. (2011). 'The puzzle of migrant labor shortage and rural labor surplus in China'. *China Economic Review*, 22, 585–600.

Knight, J., Deng, Q., and Li, S. (2017). 'China's expansion of higher education: The labor market consequences of a supply shock'. *China Economic Review*, 43, 127–41.

Knight, J., and Ding, S. (2012). *China's Remarkable Economic Growth*, Oxford: Oxford University Press.

Knight, J., and Gunatilaka, R. (2011). 'Does economic growth raise happiness in China?' *Oxford Development Studies*, 39(1), 1–34.

Knight, J., and Li, S. (2005). 'Wages, firm profitability, and labour market segmentation in urban China'. *China Economic Review*, 16, 2015–28.

Knight, J., Li, S., and Song, L. (2006). 'The rural–urban divide and the evolution of political economy in China'. In J. Boyce, S. Cullenberg, P. Pattanaik, and R. Pollin (eds.), *Human Development in the Era of Globalisation: Essays in Honor of Keith B. Griffin*, 44–62, Northampton, MA: Edward Elgar.

Knight, J., Li, S., and Wan, H. (2022). 'Why has China's inequality of household wealth risen rapidly in the twenty-first century? *Review of Income and Wealth*, 68(1), 109–38.

Knight, J., Ma, B., and Gunatilaka, R. (2022). 'The puzzle of falling happiness despite rising income in rural China: Eleven hypotheses'. *Economic Development and Cultural Change*, 70(3), 1103–31.

Knight, J., and Song, L. (1999). *The Rural-Urban Divide: Economic Disparities and Interactions in China*, Oxford: Oxford University Press.

Knight, J., and Song, L. (2005). *Towards a Labour Market in China*, Oxford: Oxford University Press.

Knight, J., and Song, L. (2008). 'China's emerging urban wage structure, 1995-2002'. In B. Gustafsson, S. Li, and T. Sicular (eds.), *Inequality and Public Policy in China*, 221–42, New York: Cambridge University Press.

Kristjánsson, A. S. (2011). 'Income redistribution in Iceland: Development and European comparisons'. *European Journal of Social Security*, 13(40), 392–423.

Lewis, W. A. (1954). 'Economic development with unlimited supplies of labor'. *The Manchester School*, 22(2), 139–91.

Li, S., and Sato, H. (eds.) (2006). *Unemployment, Inequality, and Poverty in Urban China*, Oxon: Routledge.

Li, S., Sato, H., and Sicular, T. (eds.) (2013). *Rising Inequality in China: Challenges to a Harmonious Society*, New York: Cambridge University Press.

Li, S., and Wan, H. (2015). 'Evolution of wealth inequality in China'. *China Economic Journal*, 8(3), 264–87.

Li, S., and Zhao R. (2007). 'Changes in the distribution of wealth in China 1995–2002'. Working Paper Series UNU-WIDER Research Paper, World Institute for Development Economic Research (UNU-WIDER).

Li, S., and Zhao, R. (eds.) (2020). *Research on China's Income Distribution and Labor Market*, Beijing: China Labor and Social Security Press.

Liang, Z., Appleton, S., and Song, L. (2016). 'Informal employment in China: Trends, patterns, and determinants of entry'. IZA Discussion Paper No. 10129, August: 1–23.

Mahler, V. A., and Jesuit, D. K. (2006). 'Fiscal redistribution in the developed countries: New insights from the Luxembourg income study'. *Socio-Economic Review*, 4(3), 483–511.

Maurer-Fazio, M. (2012). 'Ethnic discrimination in China's internet job board labor market, *IZA Journal of Migration*, 1(12). www.izajom.com/content/1/1/12.

Meng, X., Gregory, R., and Wang, Y. (2005). 'Poverty, inequality, and growth in urban China, 1986–2000'. *Journal of Comparative Economics*, 33(4), 710–29.

Milanovic, B. (2000). 'The median-voter hypothesis, income inequality, and income redistribution: An empirical test with the required data'. *European Journal of Political Economy*, 16(3), 367–410.

Milanovic, B., and Yitzhaki, S. (2002). 'Decomposing world income inequality: Does the world have a middle class?' *Review of Income and Wealth*, 48, 155–78.

Mohapatra, S., Rozelle, S., and Goodhue, R. (2007). 'The rise of self-employment in rural China: Development or distress?' *World Development*, 35(1), 163–81.

Mullaney, T. S. (2011). *Coming to Terms with the Nation: Ethnic Classification in Modern China*, Berkeley: University of California Press.

National Bureau of Statistics. (2021). *Statistical Yearbook*, Beijing.

Naughton, B. (2018). *The Chinese Economy: Adaption and Growth*, 2nd ed., Cambridge, MA: MIT Press.

Park, A., and Wang, S. (2010). 'Community-based development and poverty alleviation: An evaluation of China's poor village investment program'. *Journal of Public Economics*, 94(9–10), 790–9.

Piketty, T., Yang, L. and Zucman, G. (2019). 'Capital accumulation, private property, and rising inequality in China, 1978–2015'. *American Economic Review*, 109(7), 2469–96.

Plotnick, R. (1981). 'A measure of horizontal inequity'. *Review of Economics and Statistics*, 63(2), 283–8.

Riskin, C., Zhao, R., and Li, S. (eds.) (2001). *China's Retreat from Equality: Income Distribution and Economic Transition*, New York: M. E. Sharpe.

Roemer, J. (1996). *Theories of Social Justice*, Harvard: Harvard University Press.

Shen, Y., and Alkire, S. (2022). 'Exploring China's potential child poverty'. *China & World Economy*, 30(1), 82–105.

Sicular, T., Li, S., Yue, S., and Sato, H. (eds.) (2020). *Changing Trends in China's Inequality: Evidence, Analysis, and Prospects*, New York: Oxford University Press.

Sicular, T., Ximing, Y., Gustafsson, B., and Shi, L. (2007). 'The rural urban income gap and inequality in China'. *Review of Income and Wealth*, 53(1), 93–126.

Sicular, T., Yang, X., and Gustafsson, B. (2022). 'The rise of China's global middle class in international perspective'. *China & World Economy*, 30(1), 5–27.

Wan, H., Gustafsson, B., and Wang, Y. (2022). 'Convergence of inequality dimensions in China: Income, consumption, and wealth from 1988 to 2018'. Paper presented at the IZA workshop Inequality in Post-Transition and Emerging Economies, 27 and 28 October 2022.

Wan, H., and Knight, J. (2023). 'China's growing but slowing inequality of household wealth: A challenge to "common prosperity" ?'. *China Economic Review*, 79, 101947.

World Bank. (2018). *World Governance Report 2018*, Washington, DC: World Bank.

World Bank and Development Research Center of the State Council of the People's Republic of China. (2013). 'Equality of opportunity and basic security for all'. *Supporting Report 4 to China 2030: Building a Modern Harmonious, and Creative Society*, 271–359. https://doi.org/10.1596/9780821395455_CH04.

Xiao, W., and Wu, M. (2021). 'Life-cycle factors and entrepreneurship: Evidence from rural China'. *Small Business Economics*, 57, 2017–40.

Yang, X., Gustafsson, B., and Sicular, T. (2021). 'Inequality of opportunity in household income, China 2002–2018'. *China Economic Review*, 69, October, 101684.

Ye, L., Tim, G., and Li, S. (2020). 'Compliance with legal minimum wages and overtime pay in China: Effects across the distribution of wages'. In S. Li, and C. Lin (eds.), *Minimum Wages in China*, 223–57, Singapore: Palgrave Macmillan.

Yue, X., and Zhang, X. (2021) (in Chinese). 'Reflections on optimizing the income distribution effect of tax revenue'. *Taxation Research*, 37(4), 11–18.

Zhang, J. (2021). 'A survey on income inequality in China'. *Journal of Economic Literature*, 59(4), 1191–239.

Zhang, X., Yue, X., and Shao, G. (2020) (in Chinese). 'An international comparison of redistribution effects of personal income tax'. *International Taxation in China*, 33(7), 18–24.

Cambridge Elements ≡

Development Economics

Series Editor-in-Chief
Kunal Sen
UNU-WIDER and University of Manchester

Kunal Sen, UNU-WIDER Director, is Editor-in-Chief of the Cambridge Elements in Development Economics series. Professor Sen has over three decades of experience in academic and applied development economics research, and has carried out extensive work on international finance, the political economy of inclusive growth, the dynamics of poverty, social exclusion, female labour force participation, and the informal sector in developing economies. His research has focused on India, East Asia, and sub-Saharan Africa.

In addition to his work as Professor of Development Economics at the University of Manchester, Kunal has been the Joint Research Director of the Effective States and Inclusive Development (ESID) Research Centre, and a Research Fellow at the Institute for Labor Economics (IZA). He has also served in advisory roles with national governments and bilateral and multilateral development agencies, including the UK's Department for International Development, Asian Development Bank, and the International Development Research Centre.

Thematic Editors
Tony Addison
University of Copenhagen and UNU-WIDER

Tony Addison is a Professor of Economics in the University of Copenhagen's Development Economics Research Group. He is also a Non-Resident Senior Research Fellow at UNU-WIDER, Helsinki, where he was previously the Chief Economist-Deputy Director. In addition, he is Professor of Development Studies at the University of Manchester. His research interests focus on the extractive industries, energy transition, and macroeconomic policy for development.

Chris Barret
Johnson College of Business, Cornell University

Chris Barrett is an agricultural and development economist at Cornell University. He is the Stephen B. and Janice G. Ashley Professor of Applied Economics and Management; and International Professor of Agriculture at the Charles H. Dyson School of Applied Economics and Management.He is also an elected Fellow of the American Association for the Advancement of Science, the Agricultural and Applied Economics Association, and the African Association of Agricultural Economists.

Carlos Gradín
University of Vigo

Carlos Gradín is a professor of applied economics at the University of Vigo. His main research interest is the study of inequalities, with special attention to those that exist between population groups (e.g., by race or sex). His publications have contributed to improving the empirical evidence in developing and developed countries, as well as globally, and to improving the available data and methods used.

Rachel M. Gisselquist
UNU-WIDER

Rachel M. Gisselquist is a Senior Research Fellow and member of the Senior Management Team of UNU-WIDER. She specializes in the comparative politics of developing countries, with particular attention to issues of inequality, ethnic and identity politics, foreign aid and state building, democracy and governance, and sub-Saharan African politics. Dr Gisselquist has edited a dozen collections in these areas, and her articles are published in a range of leading journals.

Shareen Joshi
Georgetown University

Shareen Joshi is an Associate Professor of International Development at Georgetown University's School of Foreign Service in the United States. Her research focuses on issues of inequality, human capital investment and grassroots collective action in South Asia. Her work has been published in the fields of development economics, population studies, environmental studies and gender studies.

Patricia Justino
UNU-WIDER and IDS – UK

Patricia Justino is a Senior Research Fellow at UNU-WIDER and Professorial Fellow at the Institute of Development Studies (IDS) (on leave). Her research focuses on the relationship between political violence, governance and development outcomes. She has published widely in the fields of development economics and political economy and is the co-founder and co-director of the Households in Conflict Network (HiCN).

Marinella Leone
University of Pavia

Marinella Leone is an assistant professor at the Department of Economics and Management, University of Pavia, Italy. She is an applied development economist. Her more recent research focuses on the study of early child development parenting programmes, on education, and gender-based violence. In previous research she investigated the short-, long-term and intergenerational impact of conflicts on health, education and domestic violence. She has published in top journals in economics and development economics.

Jukka Pirttilä
University of Helsinki and UNU-WIDER

Jukka Pirttilä is Professor of Public Economics at the University of Helsinki and VATT Institute for Economic Research. He is also a Non-Resident Senior Research Fellow at UNU-WIDER. His research focuses on tax policy, especially for developing countries. He is a co-principal investigator at the Finnish Centre of Excellence in Tax Systems Research.

Andy Sumner
King's College London and UNU-WIDER

Andy Sumner is Professor of International Development at King's College London; a Non-Resident Senior Fellow at UNU-WIDER and a Fellow of the Academy of Social Sciences. He has published extensively in the areas of poverty, inequality, and economic development.

About the Series

Cambridge Elements in Development Economics is led by UNU-WIDER in partnership with Cambridge University Press. The series publishes authoritative studies on important topics in the field covering both micro and macro aspects of development economics.

United Nations University World Institute for Development Economics Research

United Nations University World Institute for Development Economics Research (UNU-WIDER) provides economic analysis and policy advice aiming to promote sustainable and equitable development for all. The institute began operations in 1985 in Helsinki, Finland, as the first research centre of the United Nations University. Today, it is one of the world's leading development economics think tanks, working closely with a vast network of academic researchers and policy makers, mostly based in the Global South.

Cambridge Elements

Development Economics

Printed in the United States
by Baker & Taylor Publisher Services